Exploring
TUNISIAN CROCHET

LORI HARRISON

STACKPOLE BOOKS

Essex, Connecticut
Blue Ridge Summit, Pennsylvania

STACKPOLE BOOKS

An imprint of Globe Pequot, the trade division of The Rowman & Littlefield
Publishing Group, Inc.
4501 Forbes Blvd., Ste. 200
Lanham, MD 20706
www.rowman.com

Distributed by NATIONAL BOOK NETWORK
800-462-6420

Copyright © 2023 by Lori Harrison

Designs: Lori Harrison (Aklori Designs)
Tech Editor: Sharon Carter (Dragonhill Studios)
Photography: Stefan O'Dougherty and Lori Harrison

British Library Cataloguing in Publication Information available

Library of Congress Cataloging-in-Publication Data

Names: Harrison, Lori, 1978– author.
Title: Exploring Tunisian crochet / Lori Harrison.
Description: Essex, Connecticut : Stackpole Books, [2023]
Identifiers: LCCN 2023002115 (print) | LCCN 2023002116 (ebook) | ISBN
  9780811772235 (paperback) | ISBN 9780811772242 (epub)
Subjects: LCSH: Crocheting—Patterns. | Crocheting—Tunisia.
Classification: LCC TT819.T8 H37 2023 (print) | LCC TT819.T8 (ebook) |
  DDC 746.43/4041—dc23/eng/20230224
LC record available at https://lccn.loc.gov/2023002115
LC ebook record available at https://lccn.loc.gov/2023002116

♾™ The paper used in this publication meets the minimum requirements of
American National Standard for Information Sciences—Permanence of Paper for
Printed Library Materials, ANSI/NISO Z39.48-1992.

First Edition

This book is dedicated
to my partner, Stefan.
Without his endless support
and encouragement, this book
would not have been possible.
Thank you, my love!

Contents

Venturing beyond the Basics: Modified Stitches and Variations 35

Intermediate and Advanced Techniques 41

How to Read a Pattern 53

PATTERNS

Introduction

Tunisian crochet is a style of crochet that has been around for over one hundred years and has gone by many names (afghan crochet, tricot crochet, railroad knitting, hybrid crochet, to name a few), but only in recent years has it started to be explored beyond the basic stitches. Modern Tunisian crochet is so much more than thick bulky blankets and is now used for everything from stylish garments to fancy lace shawls. This book will guide you on your Tunisian crochet journey from the beginnings of hook selection to building up advanced techniques and solutions to common problems.

My Tunisian crochet journey started with a trip to my local yarn store. As I was perusing the yarn, one of the salespersons was showing another customer a scarf in a texture I had never seen before. I was intrigued and had to know what technique was used to create this gorgeous texture. I left the shop with my first Tunisian crochet hook (a 12-inch straight 6 mm J-10 hook) and a strong desire to learn more. I quickly became obsessed and absorbed all the information I could find in books and online but quickly ran out of resources.

While this book assumes no prior knowledge of crochet or Tunisian crochet, it is designed to guide you well beyond the basics. There are comprehensive tutorials for stitch variations, shaping, and other advanced techniques. The patterns in the second part of the book then use these stitches and techniques so they are not abstract concepts. The designs start at the most basic (perfect for your first Tunisian crochet project while not being boring) and gradually increase in difficulty, ending with an intricate lace shawl. Every pattern has hints and suggestions to give you confidence and help guide you on your journey to become an advanced Tunisian crocheter.

When I started designing, it was because I wanted patterns that pushed the boundaries of what Tunisian crochet had to offer at the time. I kept pushing and designing, and I am still finding new concepts to explore. I designed my first pattern featuring cables for this book and can't wait to create more.

I hope this book inspires you on your Tunisian crochet journey. So are you ready? Grab your hook and let's start exploring!

Lori

Getting Started

TUNISIAN CROCHET HOOKS AND TOOLS

Before getting started, you'll need to assemble the right tools. You can begin your journey with just a regular crochet hook for practicing the stitches and techniques as well as the first few patterns in this book. However, you'll quickly find that many Tunisian crochet patterns will require a Tunisian crochet hook.

What Is a Tunisian Crochet Hook?

Similar to knitting, Tunisian crochet requires holding multiple active stitches on the hook simultaneously. This is why Tunisian crochet hooks resemble knitting needles with a hook at the end. The shaft needs to be of uniform thickness so that the stitches are all the same size. Tunisian crochet hooks come in several varieties: straight hooks, hooks with cables, interchangeable hooks, and double-ended hooks.

Tunisian crochet patterns that are worked flat are the most common and use single hooks. These hooks can be long straight hooks, hooks with fixed cable, or an interchangeable hook with cable. The hook must be long enough to hold all the stitches in the longest row of the pattern.

STRAIGHT HOOKS

Straight hooks have a long uniform shaft and a stopper at the end. Patterns with a limited number of stitches, like scarves and blanket squares, can be done with a straight hook. A straight hook can be used for many projects, but it can be hard on the wrist if the design has shaping. A straight hook holds the entire weight of the fabric on the hook, which can be tiring.

Straight hooks

CABLED HOOKS

A cabled hook is typically a short straight hook with an attached cable. Patterns with rows that have shaping or a large number of stitches often require a hook with a cable. A cabled hook can be easier on the hands and wrists because not all the weight of the fabric is held on the hook. Cabled hooks come with either a fixed cord or interchangeable cords. Hooks with fixed cables tend to be very long to accommodate any pattern. Interchangeable hooks make it convenient to choose the cable length to match your pattern.

DOUBLE-ENDED HOOKS

Tunisian crochet patterns that are worked in the round use double-ended hooks. These have a hook on each end. Two hooks joined with a cable can also be used for in-the-round projects. It is important to note that both hooks need to be the same size. Straight double-ended hooks work best for smaller projects like hats. For larger projects, such as garments or cowls, using two hooks joined with a cable allows you to work more forward pass stitches before having to work the return pass.

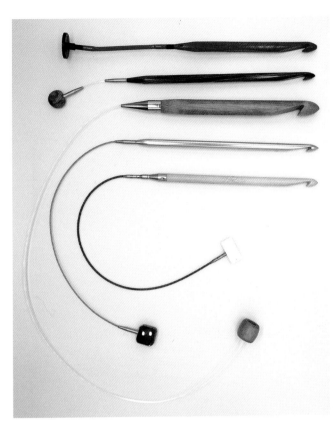

Cabled hooks

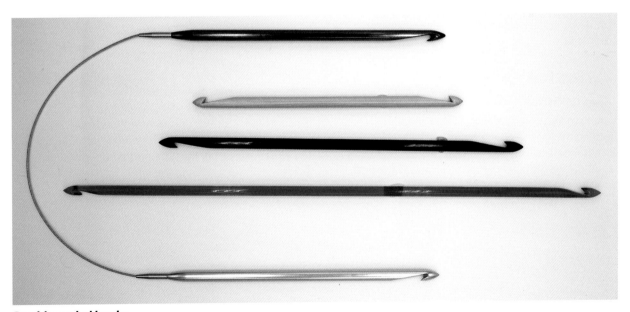

Double-ended hooks

Hook Size

The most important thing to know when choosing a hook is that the hook needs to be at least one to two sizes larger than what the yarn band suggests for regular crochet or knitting. For example, a typical sock/fingering/superfine yarn Tunisian crochet pattern will require a 4.5 mm (G-7) or 5 mm (H-8) hook. Using a hook that is too small will create a very dense fabric that is hard to work, has no drape, and comes with a lot of curl. If you're finding Tunisian crocheting uncomfortable, try a bigger hook.

Hook Attributes

Tunisian crochet hooks come in a wide variety of materials and shapes. Choosing among them is mostly a matter of preference. Metal and laminated wood hooks tend to be smoother than bamboo or plastic, which tend to be grippy. A hook with a pointed head can be easier to insert when working a stitch. A cable that swivels can be easier on the wrists. There is no one hook that is best for everyone; it is important to find the style that works best for you so that crocheting is enjoyable.

Holding the Hook

Hold the hook between the thumb and fingers of your dominant hand with the shaft resting against your palm. Use your nondominant hand to hold the fabric and the yarn.

Hold the hook in your dominant hand and the fabric and yarn in your nondominant hand.

Other Tools

Removable stitch markers, scissors, a ruler or tape measure, and a tapestry needle are useful to have readily available.

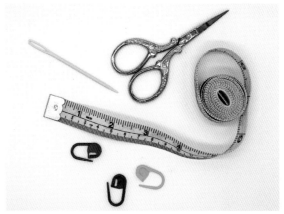

Clockwise from top left: tapestry needle, scissors, tape measure, stitch markers

TUNISIAN CROCHET HOOK SIZES

Yarn Weight	Yarn Name	Regular Crochet Hook Size (mm)	Tunisian Crochet Hook Size (mm)
0–Lace	Lace	1.4–1.6 mm	3–5 mm
1–Superfine	Sock, Fingering, Baby	2.25–3.5 mm	4–5 mm
2–Fine	Sport, Baby	3.5–4.5 mm	4.5–5.5 mm
3–Light	DK, Light Worsted	4.5–5.5 mm	5.5–7 mm
4–Medium	Worsted, Aran	5.5–6.5 mm	6–8 mm
5–Bulky	Chunky	6.5–9 mm	8–11 mm
6–Super Bulky	Super Bulky	9–15 mm	11–15 mm
7–Jumbo	Jumbo, Roving	15+ mm	15+ mm

BEGINNING YOUR TUNISIAN CROCHET JOURNEY

Now that you have selected your hook, we can begin learning the fundamentals of Tunisian crochet, starting with Tunisian crochet row and stitch anatomy. All these basics can be practiced with a regular crochet hook if you limit the number of stitches in a row (start with 10). *Reminder:* Select a hook size that is at least two sizes bigger than the yarn band recommends. Grab a hook and some yarn, and let's get started.

TUNISIAN CROCHET ROWS

There are three types of rows in Tunisian crochet: foundation row, standard row, and bind-off row. A Tunisian crochet project starts with a foundation row, where the number of stitches is established for the first row of the project. Standard rows are the main part of the pattern and can be any combination of Tunisian crochet stitches. The final row of any pattern is the bind-off row, which closes the last standard row of stitches.

Forward and Return Passes

Every row in Tunisian crochet (except the bind-off row) consists of two parts: a forward pass and a return pass. On the forward pass, you add loops to the hook by working the stitches in the row. On the return pass, you close the stitches and remove loops from the hook. In general, you do not turn your work. Both the forward and the return passes are done with the front side of the fabric facing you. At the end of the return pass, there is one loop on your hook, which is the first loop on the hook for the next row.

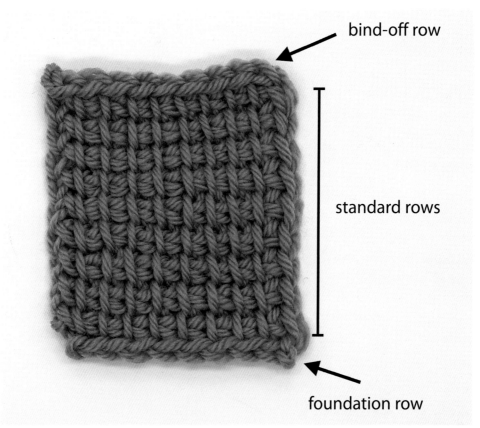

bind-off row

standard rows

foundation row

Tunisian crochet begins with a foundation row, has as many standard rows as desired, and finishes with a bind-off row.

FOUNDATION ROW

The first row in Tunisian crochet is always the foundation row. The most common way to start a Tunisian crochet foundation row is with a chain.

1. Start the chain by creating a slipknot. Wrap the yarn around the hook with the tail end on top.

2. Wrap the yarn around the hook. This is called a yarn over (yo).

3. Use the hook to pull the yarn through the first loop and tighten. There is now 1 loop on the hook.

4. Yarn over.

5. Pull yarn over through the loop on hook. This is a chain stitch.

6. Repeat steps 4 and 5 until the required number of chains is complete. This will be the base for the foundation row.

The next step in creating the foundation row is to pick up loops in the back bumps of the chain.

7. Always skip the first chain from the hook. The photo shows where the first loop will be picked up.

8. Insert the hook under the back bump of the second chain from the hook.

9. Yarn over.

10. Pull loop through the chain and leave loop on hook.

11. Continue picking up a loop in the back bump of each remaining chain. The number of loops on the hook will be the same as the number of starting chains.

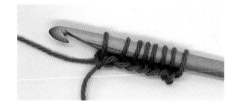

Foundation Row Return Pass

After all the required loops are on the hook, work the return pass. Do not turn the fabric.

1. The foundation row return pass starts with a chain 1 (yarn over and pull through 1 loop).

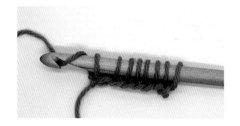

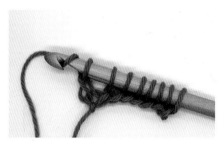

2. Yarn over and pull through 2 loops.

3. Repeat *yarn over and pull through 2 loops* until all stitches have been closed and there is only 1 loop left on the hook. The loop remaining on the hook is now the first loop on your hook for the first row.

STITCH ANATOMY

Once the foundation row is finished, the first standard row is where the fun begins. Every Tunisian crochet stitch consists of 5 bars: 2 vertical bars and 3 horizontal bars.

1. **Front vertical bar:** The front vertical bar is often simply referred to as the vertical bar. It is in the front of the stitch and to the left of the back vertical bar.

2. **Back vertical bar:** The back vertical bar is behind and to the right of the front vertical bar.

3. **Top horizontal bar:** The top horizontal bar is to the front of the 3 horizontal bars.

4. **Back horizontal bar:** The back horizontal bar is the back bump of the return pass. It is directly over the vertical bars.

5. **Bottom horizontal bar:** The bottom horizontal bar is below and behind the top and back horizontal bars.

All of these bars can be worked in a variety of ways, giving Tunisian crochet its unique textures.

TUNISIAN SIMPLE STITCH (TSS)

The Tunisian simple stitch is the most common Tunisian crochet stitch and will be the first stitch on our journey.

Note: When stitch instructions differ for right-handed and left-handed makers, a separate box will give left-handed instructions.

1. Rows in Tunisian crochet start with 1 loop on the hook. The first set of vertical bars is skipped, and the first stitch of the row is worked into the second set of vertical bars. The photo shows where the first stitch will be worked.

2. To create the Tunisian simple stitch (Tss), insert the hook behind the front vertical bar from right to left.

3. Yarn over.

4. Pull up a loop and leave loop on hook.

5. Continue working each set of vertical bars until only 1 set remains.

FOR LEFT-HANDED MAKERS

Tss step 2: Insert the hook behind the front vertical bar from left to right.

TUNISIAN EDGE STITCH (TE)

Unlike all other stitches in the forward pass, the last stitch has 3 vertical bars. While this last stitch can be worked the same as for the Tunisian simple stitch, working a Tunisian edge stitch will create a nicer, neater edge.

1. Insert the hook behind the outer 2 vertical bars.

2. Yarn over and pull up a loop.

STANDARD RETURN PASS

After every forward pass, there is a return pass. While the standard return pass is the most common, return passes can also have increases and decreases. When a nonstandard return pass is used, it will be explained in the pattern.

The standard return pass (RP) is as follows: chain 1, *yarn over and pull through 2 loops; repeat from * until there is only 1 loop on the hook.

Completed standard return pass

BIND-OFF ROW

After the last standard row of the pattern has been completed, a bind-off row is required so the fabric doesn't look unfinished. The two most common bind-off stitches are the slip stitch bind-off (slstBO) and the single crochet bind-off (scBO).

Slip Stitch Bind-off (slstBO)

The slip stitch bind-off with Tunisian simple stitch is the most common bind-off.

1. Insert the hook for stitch indicated (shown for Tss).

2. Yarn over and pull the loop through the stitch.

3. Slip stitch by pulling the loop from step 2 through the first loop on hook. One loop remains on the hook.

4. Repeat steps 1–3 until all stitches have been worked.

Single Crochet Bind-off (scBO)

A single crochet bind-off gives a stretchier edge compared to the slip stitch bind-off.

1. Insert the hook for stitch indicated (shown for Tss) and pull up a loop.

2. Yarn over.

3. Pull through both loops on hook.

4. Repeat steps 1–3 until all stitches have been worked.

Any Tunisian crochet stitch can be used for the bind-off (the prior examples used the Tss). Instead of inserting the hook as for Tss in step 1, insert the hook for the desired stitch, and then continue with steps 2–4.

Basic Stitches

In addition to the Tunisian simple stitch, there are four other basic Tunisian crochet stitches: Tunisian purl stitch, Tunisian knit stitch, Tunisian reverse stitch, and Tunisian full stitch.

TUNISIAN PURL STITCH (TPS)

The Tunisian purl stitch is so named because it resembles the purl stitch in knitting. Tunisian purl stitch is worked behind the front vertical bar just like Tunisian simple stitch. The difference is that the yarn is held in front of the fabric.

Tunisian purl stitch

1. Bring the yarn to the front of the fabric. Insert the hook from right to left behind the front vertical bar.

2. Yarn over.

3. Pull up a loop, leave loop on hook.

FOR LEFT-HANDED MAKERS

Tps step 1: Bring the yarn to the front of the fabric. Insert the hook behind the front vertical bar from left to right.

TUNISIAN KNIT STITCH (TKS)

The Tunisian knit stitch is so named because it resembles the knit stitch in knitting.

Tunisian knit stitch

1. Insert the hook from front to back, between the 2 vertical bars.

2. With the yarn held behind the fabric, yarn over.

3. Pull up a loop. Leave loop on hook.

TUNISIAN REVERSE STITCH (TRS)

Tunisian reverse stitch is so named because it is worked on the reverse (or back side) of the fabric.

Tunisian reverse stitch

1. With your hook behind the fabric, insert the hook from right to left behind the back vertical bar.

2. Yarn over.

3. Pull up a loop. Leave loop on hook.

FOR LEFT-HANDED MAKERS

Trs step 1: Insert the hook behind the back vertical bar from left to right.

TUNISIAN FULL STITCH (TFS)

While all the other basic stitches have been made by inserting the hook into the vertical bars, the Tunisian full stitch is worked between 2 sets of vertical bars and under the 3 horizontal bars.

Tunisian full stitch

1. Insert the hook under all 3 horizontal bars.

2. Yarn over.

3. Pull up a loop. Leave the loop on the hook.

Note: If you're working a swatch of Tfs, there is 1 more set of horizontal bars compared to vertical bars. If you work under all of them, your swatch will gradually grow by 1 stitch per row. To create a square swatch, alternate rows of skipping either the first or the last set of horizontal bars.

Basic Techniques

Once the fundamental concepts of Tunisian crochet have been mastered, it is time to learn shaping and other techniques necessary to be able to create patterns beyond rectangular swatches. This chapter will cover how to add and subtract stitches from a row, changing colors, joining two fabrics together as you go, and finishing techniques, as well as tips and tricks for dealing with common problems.

INCREASES

There are several methods for adding stitches to a row in Tunisian crochet. One of the most common ways to increase is to add a stitch between stitches on the forward pass, such as a yarn over or a Tunisian full stitch. Increases can also be created by working multiple stitches into 1 stitch space or adding stitch spaces on the return.

Tunisian Full Stitch Increase

In these photos a Tunisian full stitch is worked between the first and second Tunisian simple stitches in the row to increase the stitch count of each row by one.

1. Work a Tss in the second set of vertical bars in the row.

2. Work a Tfs before the next set of vertical bars.

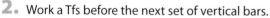

3. Work a Tss in the third set of vertical bars.

Yarn Over Increase

A yarn over can be added between any 2 stitches. Multiple yarn overs can be done at once. **_Note:_** With multiple consecutive yarn overs, close each stitch individually on the return pass.

1. Work a yarn over after the first Tss in the row.

2. Work a Tss into the next set of vertical bars.

Back Bar Increase

Work a stitch into the back bar of the return pass between the second and third sets of vertical bars.

Back bar increase

Multiple Stitches Worked in 1 Stitch

Working 2 or more stitches into 1 stitch is a method for adding stitches that is especially useful when more than 1 increase is required at a single location. In order to work multiple stitches into the same stitch, consecutive stitches cannot be the same stitch, but any number of stitches can be worked into a single stitch.

2 STITCHES WORKED INTO 1 SET OF VERTICAL BARS

In this example, both a Tss and a modified Tss are worked into the same stitch. The notation for this is (Tss, Tmss).

1. A Tss is worked into the third set of vertical bars.

2. A modified Tss (see page 35) is also worked into the third set of vertical bars.

MORE THAN 2 STITCHES WORKED INTO 1 SET OF VERTICAL BARS

In this example, 3 stitches are worked into a single stitch for an increase of 2 stitches. The notation for this is (Tss, Tks, Tss).

1. Three stitches will be worked into the next stitch.

2. Insert the hook for a Tss stitch.

3. Yarn over and pull up a loop.

4. Insert the hook for a Tks stitch.

5. Pull up a loop; 2 stitches have now been worked.

6. Repeat steps 2 and 3. All 3 stitches have now been worked.

21

Return Pass Increase

Increases can also be added on the return pass. This is done by adding chain stitches between the "yarn over and pull through 2 loops" and, in the next forward pass, by pulling up a loop in the back bump of the extra chain.

1. A chain stitch is added on the return pass of the prior row.

2. On the forward pass, pull up a loop in the back bump of the chain.

3. A Tss is worked in the next set of vertical bars.

DECREASES

Just like increases, there are multiple ways to decrease the number of stitches in a row. The most common decrease technique is to work 2 or more stitches together on the forward pass. Other methods for decreasing include closing multiple stitches together on the return pass or simply skipping a stitch (sk st).

Forward Pass Decrease

Decreasing on the forward pass is done by inserting the hook in the next 2 or more sets of vertical bars and pulling up a single loop.

DECREASE 2 STITCHES TOGETHER

1. This swatch has a Tss2Tog decrease at the start of the forward pass.

2. Insert the hook as for Tss behind the next 2 sets of vertical bars.

3. Yarn over and pull through both sets of bars.

DECREASE 3 STITCHES TOGETHER

1. This swatch has 2 decreases at a single location. The decrease is a Tss 3 stitches together (Tss3Tog) and is in the middle of each row.

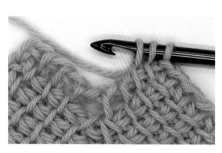

2. Insert the hook as for Tss behind the next 3 sets of vertical bars.

3. Yarn over and pull through all 3 sets of bars.

Decreases on the forward pass can be done for all basic stitches worked into the vertical bars. For Tps2Tog or Trs2Tog, insert the hook as for Tps or Trs in the next 2 stitches, and then yarn over and pull up a loop. For Tks2Tog, insert the hook behind the first set of vertical bars as for Tss and into the second set as for Tks, and then yarn over and pull up a loop.

Return Pass Decrease

Decreasing on the return pass can be done at any point during the return pass by closing more than one stitch at the same time. It is important to note that on the next forward pass, you'll treat the stitches that were decreased together as a single stitch.

DECREASE AT THE END OF THE RETURN PASS

1. Work the return pass until there are 3 loops left on the hook.

2. Yarn over and pull through 3 loops.

3. In the next forward pass, do not work either of the first 2 sets of vertical bars. The first stitch is worked into the third set of bars.

DECREASE IN THE MIDDLE OF THE RETURN PASS.

1. In this swatch, 3 stitches are closed together during the return pass.

2. Work a standard return pass prior to the decrease.

3. Yarn over; pull through 4 loops.

4. On the next forward pass, treat the 3 stitches as a single stitch. Insert the hook behind all 3 vertical bars.

5. Yarn over and pull up a single loop.

DECREASE AT THE BEGINNING OF THE RETURN PASS.

Decreasing at the beginning of the return pass is a special case because, instead of pulling through extra loops, you simply do not chain 1 at the beginning of the return pass.

1. Work the forward pass as normal.

2. Do not chain 1.

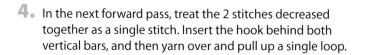

3. Yarn over; pull through 2 loops. Notice how the last 2 stitches of the forward pass do not have a return pass stitch between them.

4. In the next forward pass, treat the 2 stitches decreased together as a single stitch. Insert the hook behind both vertical bars, and then yarn over and pull up a single loop.

COLOR CHANGES

Tunisian crochet is unique in that each row has 2 passes. This feature creates noticeably different effects depending on where the color change occurs.

Creating Stripes

If the desired result is stripes, the swap between yarn colors occurs at the end of the return pass. Remember that the loop created at the last "yarn over and pull through 2 loops" of the return pass is the first loop on the next forward pass. To create a row with loops all the same color, the color change happens just before the last "yarn over and pull through 2 loops" of the return pass in the prior row.

1. Stop working the return pass when there are 2 loops on the hook. Drop the current color and pick up the next color. Yarn over.

2. Pull through 2 loops. Loop on hook is in the new color. Continue working the next forward pass.

3. Repeat steps 1 and 2 whenever a color change is required.

Blending and Fading

Having a forward pass and a return pass allows for very smooth color transitions. If the colors are swapped at the end of the forward pass, both colors contribute to the row; the result is a mixing of the two colors. This method of blending yarn makes skein transitions unnoticeable and can create a smoother fade compared to knit or crochet. The first photo shows how both colors contribute to each row.

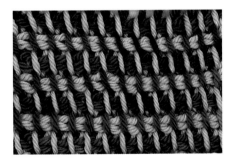

1. Work the entire forward pass until the last stitch.

2. Insert the hook for the edge stitch. Drop the current color and pick up the next color.

3. Yarn over with next color and pull up a loop. Continue the return pass with the new color.

Color Blocking

Color blocking occurs when the colors are swapped at the same stitch in both the forward and the return passes.

1. Work the first part of the forward pass in Color 1.

2. Drop Color 1 and work the remainder of the forward pass in Color 2.

3. Work the return pass in Color 2 until there is only 1 loop of Color 2 on the hook.

4. Pick up Color 1 and bring up behind Color 2. Twisting the 2 strands helps prevent gaps.

5. Yarn over and pull through 2 loops.

6. Continue with Color 1 until the return pass is complete. Repeat from step 1.

JOINS

Entrelac Join

The most common method of joining is the entrelac join. While this versatile join is easy, it can create gapping at the seam, but the gap is often used as a design element.

1. At the end of the forward pass, insert hook from front to back behind the edge vertical bars.

2. Yarn over.

3. Pull through. This loop acts like the chain 1 in a standard return pass.

4. Start the return pass with a yarn over and pull through 2 loops.

5. Continue the return pass as usual.

6. When working an entrelac join on the top of the fabric, insert the hook under both horizontal bars.

Seamless Edge Join

For a more invisible join, use the seamless edge join. This join can be more fiddly than an entrelac join but is useful when a gap is undesirable.

1. Insert the hook between the edge stitch vertical bars and behind the bottom horizontal bar.

2. Back side of fabric showing where the hook is inserted.

3. Yarn over and pull up a loop.

4. Continue the return pass.

FINISHING

Fasten Off

Whenever a strand of yarn is done being used, the pattern will say to "fasten off." This means to tie off the yarn and cut the strand while leaving a tail long enough to weave in comfortably, about 6 in (15 cm).

Fasten off by tying the yarn and cutting it, leaving a 6 in (15 cm) length for weaving in.

Weaving In Ends

Weaving in ends is easy to do on the back side of Tunisian crochet. Thread the tail end of the yarn into a tapestry needle and weave the end through the back horizontal bars of the return pass.

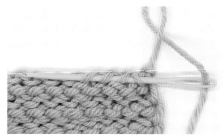

Weave in ends with a tapestry needle.

Sewing

WHIPSTITCH SEAM

Hold the 2 pieces to be sewn together such that either the back sides or the front sides of the fabric are facing each other. Insert the tapestry needle through both pieces of fabric from front to back and pull the yarn through, leaving enough of a tail to weave in when finished. Bring the tapestry needle to the front and repeat until the entire edge has been sewn.

MATTRESS STITCH SEAM

Place the 2 pieces of fabric side by side with both front sides facing up. Starting at the bottom stitch of the right fabric, insert the tapestry needle behind the vertical bars from bottom to top. Pull the yarn through, leaving a long tail to weave in when finished. Next, insert the tapestry needle in the first stitch of the left fabric from bottom to top behind the vertical bars. While alternating sides, repeat until all stitches along the seam have been sewn. Pull the yarn tight to bring the 2 pieces of fabric together.

DEALING WITH COMMON PROBLEMS

Eliminating Curl

Tunisian crochet fabric has a strong tendency to curl. Light curling is expected and can be fixed with blocking. If the fabric has anything more than light curling, the hook is too small for the yarn. Reminder: Tunisian crochet requires a bigger hook than the yarn band states. Increase the hook size until the fabric has only a small amount of curl. In the photo on the right, the same swatch using Tunisian simple stitch was created using three different hook sizes. The top swatch was made with a 5 mm hook and has heavy curling. The middle swatch was made with a 6 mm hook and has light curling that can easily be removed with blocking. The bottom swatch was made with a 6.5 mm hook and has very light curling.

Some Tunisian crochet stitches are also more prone to curling. The Tunisian knit stitch is a shorter stitch, which causes it to pull the fabric forward. A row or two of either Tunisian reverse stitch or Tunisian purl stitch can help counter this effect. In this photo, the Tss swatch (top) and Tks swatch (bottom) were created with the same yarn and hook, but the Tks shows a much stronger curl.

Straight Edges

Getting a neat straight edge at the start of the row can be done by working the first stitch of the row (2 loops on hook) and then pulling tight on the yarn.

Pull the first stitch of the row tightly.

Getting a straight edge at the start of the return pass can be done by working the first return pass stitch (often the chain 1) and then pulling gently on the yarn to decrease the loop height to be half to three-quarters the original height.

Pull gently to decrease the loop height on the first stitch of the return pass.

Trapping Yarn

When colors are swapped frequently in a pattern, it is easier to carry the yarn on the back side of the fabric instead of fastening off each time. Carrying the yarn, however, can create long loops on the back side. To reduce the length of these loops, trap the yarn. One method that is unique to Tunisian crochet is to trap the yarn with the return pass. This example shows carrying and trapping yarn at the end of the return pass, but the same method can be used to carry it anywhere in the row.

1. Work the return pass until the point where the yarn is being carried.

2. Bring the carried yarn to the front of the fabric.

3. Complete the return pass.

4. Return the carried yarn to the back side of the fabric.

5. Work the forward pass as usual.

6. Back side of the fabric shows the trapped yarn.

Venturing beyond the Basics: Modified Stitches and Variations

The basic stitches covered so far are just the beginning. There are many variations on the basic stitches as well as almost limitless stitch patterns from combining stitches. The stitches covered here are some of the more common variations, and many are used in the patterns later in the book.

Note: Beyond the five basic stitches (Tss, Tps, Tks, Trs, Tfs), there is not a lot of standardization in naming, so you may see these with different names.

TUNISIAN SIMPLE STITCH VARIATIONS

▥ Modified Tunisian Simple Stitch (Tmss)

Modified Tss is worked similarly to a Tss, but the hook is also inserted behind the top horizontal bar before pulling up a loop.

For modified Tss, insert the hook behind the front vertical bar and the top horizontal bar.

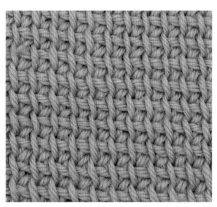

Modified Tunisian simple stitch swatch

Twisted Down Simple Stitch (Twd)

Twd is sometimes referred to as just twisted simple stitch. The twisted down simple stitch creates a twist at the top of the front vertical bar in the fabric.

Twisted down simple stitch swatch

1. The Twd stitch is created by inserting the hook behind the front vertical bar in the opposite direction from a Tss stitch.

2. The hook is then rotated clockwise (counterclockwise for left-handed makers).

3. When the hook is fully rotated, yarn over and pull up a loop.

Twisted Up Simple Stitch (Twup)

Twup is sometimes called the slanted stitch because its appearance is similar to Tss, but the vertical bars lean toward the start of the row.

Twisted up simple stitch swatch

1. The Twup stitch is created by inserting the hook behind the front vertical bar in the opposite direction from a Tss stitch.

2. The hook is then rotated counterclockwise (clockwise for left-handed makers).

3. When the hook is fully rotated, yarn over and pull up a loop.

Hint: If you're having trouble grabbing the front bar, try inserting the hook as for Tss to pull the front bar forward, remove your hook, and then work a Twup.

DIFFERENTIATING BETWEEN TWD AND TWUP

Twd and Twup are often confused. The left 2 stitches (in yellow box) in the photo are Twup and Tss. Notice how the 2 stitches pull together. This combination of stitches is often used for ribbing. The right 2 stitches (in red box) are Twd and Tss. Notice how the Twd looks like a Tss but with a twist at the top of the vertical bar.

Back Bar Tunisian Simple Stitch (Tbss)

Tbss is worked from the front side of the fabric. Insert the hook from right to left behind the back vertical bar, yarn over, and pull up a loop.

For Tbss, insert the hook behind the back vertical bar from right to left.

Back bar simple stitch swatch

FOR LEFT-HANDED MAKERS

Insert the hook from left to right behind only the back vertical bar, yarn over, and pull up a loop.

OTHER STITCH VARIATIONS

Twisted Knit Stitch (Twks)

Twks is worked similarly to a Tks, but the location of the vertical bars is swapped. Insert the hook such that the front vertical bar is to the right of the hook and the back vertical bar is to the left of the hook.

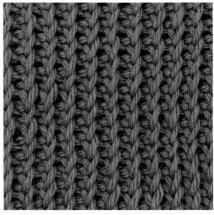

Twisted knit stitch swatch

For Twks, insert the hook with the front vertical bar to the right of the hook and the back vertical bar to the left of the hook.

FOR LEFT-HANDED MAKERS

Insert the hook such that the front vertical bar is to the left of the hook and the back vertical bar is to the right of the hook.

Reverse Tunisian Knit Stitch (Rtks)

Rtks is worked on the back side of the fabric and has a similar appearance to Trs. With the yarn in front, insert the hook from back to front between the vertical bars. Yarn over and pull up a loop.

Reverse knit stitch swatch

For Rtks, insert the hook from back to front between the vertical bars.

Purled Tunisian Reverse Stitch (Ptrs)

Ptrs is worked on the back side of the fabric. With the yarn in front, insert the hook as for Trs. Yarn over and pull up a loop.

For Ptrs, insert the hook as for Trs.

Purled reverse stitch swatch

Modified Tunisian Full Stitch (Tmfs)

Tmfs is worked by inserting the hook under the top horizontal bar and the back horizontal bar. Yarn over and pull up a loop.

For Tmfs, insert the hook under the top horizontal bar and the back horizontal bar.

Modified full stitch swatch

Tunisian Top Stitch (Ttop)

Ttop is worked by inserting the hook under the back horizontal bar. Yarn over and pull up a loop.

For Ttop, insert the hook under the back horizontal bar.

Tunisian top stitch swatch

EXTENDED STITCHES

Any stitch becomes an extended stitch simply by adding a chain 1. For example, an extended-Tss (exTss) is created by first working a Tss stitch (left photo) and then chaining 1 (right photo) and leaving the loop on the hook.

Intermediate and Advanced Techniques

MAGIC RING FOUNDATION ROW

The magic ring foundation row is a great way to start a project that grows from a point, such as a triangle shawl.

1. Start by wrapping the yarn around 2 fingers of the hand you don't use to hold your hook. Hold the tail in place with your thumb.

2. Insert the hook in the ring.

3. Pull up a loop.

4. Chain 1. Leave loop on hook.

5. Remove fingers.

6. Insert the hook into the ring again.

7. Pull up a loop.

8. Chain 1.

9. Repeat steps 6–8 until the correct number of loops is on the hook.

10. Work a standard return pass.

11. After a few rows, pull tail to tighten ring.

TUNISIAN CROCHET CABLES

A Tunisian crochet cable is one or more stitches crossing over one or more neighboring stitches (either to the immediate left or to the right). The return pass closes the stitches in their new order. The following row also works the stitches in their new order. Working Tunisian crochet cables requires a second hook, but it only needs to hold a few loops temporarily while working the cable (a regular crochet hook will work well for this step). The most common stitches used in Tunisian crochet cables are Tss and Tks.

Back Cables

With back cables, the stitches on the second hook are held to the back. Back cables lean to the right if right-handed and to the left if left-handed. To work a 6-stitch (3 over 3) back cable (3/3B) in Tss:

1. With the second hook (shown in gray), Tss in the next 3 stitches.

2. Move second hook to back of fabric and Tss in the next 3 stitches with main hook.

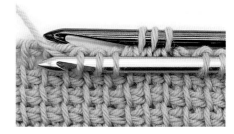

3. Keeping the second hook behind the main hook, move the second hook so that the stitches can be transferred onto the main hook.

4. Slip the stitches on the second hook to the main hook in the order they were originally worked.

5. Continue the forward pass. On the return pass, close the loops in their new order.

6. In the next forward pass, work the stitches in their new order.

Front Cables

With front cables, the loops on the second hook are held to the front. Front cables lean to the left if right-handed and to the right if left-handed. To work a 6-stitch (3 over 3) front cable (3/3F) in Tss:

1. With the second hook (shown in gray), Tss in the next 3 stitches. Hold hook in front of fabric.

2. With the main hook, Tss in next 3 stitches.

3. Keeping the second hook in front of the main hook, move the second hook so that the stitches can be transferred onto the main hook.

4. Slip the stitches on the second hook to the main hook in the order they were originally worked.

5. Remove the second hook.

6. All loops are now on main hook. Continue forward pass. On the return pass, close the stitches in this new order.

TUNISIAN CROCHET IN THE ROUND

Tunisian crochet in the round (TITR) is very similar to worked flat Tunisian crochet. The main difference between a worked flat project and a project worked in the round is that you need slightly different tools. Tunisian in the round uses a second strand of yarn and a second hook to work the return pass. Tunisian in the round uses a double-ended hook (either a straight hook with hooks on both ends or two hooks connected with a cable). It is important to note that the two hooks do need to be the same size. The other difference is that the return pass is worked with the back side of the fabric facing you. I know I said you don't turn your work in Tunisian crochet. This is the one time you do.

Tunisian crochet in the round is actually a spiral. The two ends of the fabric are joined so that there are no edge stitches. This technique is often used for hats, cowls, and garments. Tunisian crochet's unique two-pass construction can be used to create colorwork that is exclusive to Tunisian crochet in the round.

To start working in the round, you need to join the edges of your fabric. For projects that are worked entirely in the round, this often occurs at the foundation row chain or the start of the first round.

For these examples, the forward pass is worked with the silver hook and pale green yarn. The return pass is worked with the gray hook and dark green yarn.

A double-ended hook is needed for working in the round.

Joining at the Foundation Row Chain

1. Chain the required number of stitches.

2. Instead of working into the second chain from the hook, while being careful not to twist, pick up a stitch in the first back bump of the chain (end farthest from hook).

3. Pick up loops in the back bumps of the chain. Stop when it becomes difficult to work.

4. Move the loops on the hook to the second hook and turn the fabric so that the back side is facing you.

5. With the second strand of yarn, yarn over and pull up a loop.

6. Continue working the return pass just like a standard return pass. Yarn over and pull through 2 loops.

7. Stop when there are 4 loops left on hook.

8. Turn the fabric so the front side is facing you and move the loops to the first hook. Continue working the forward pass.

9. Repeat alternating between forward and return passes.

Joining after the Foundation Row Chain

Joining can occur at any point in a pattern. When this occurs, the last worked flat row uses an in-the-round return pass and the edges are joined at the start of the first round. In this example, the join is at the start of the first round immediately after the foundation row.

1. Chain the required number of stitches. Starting from the second chain from hook, pick up a loop in the back bump of all chains.

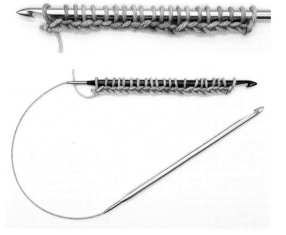

2. At this point all the foundation row loops are on the hook. Instead of working a standard return pass, a Tunisian in the round return pass is worked. Move the loops to the second hook and turn the fabric so the back side is facing you.

3. Begin the return pass by using a second strand of yarn and the second side of the double-ended hook. Yarn over.

4. Pull up a loop.

5. Continue the return pass by repeating [yarn over and pull through 2 loops] until there are 4 loops left on hook.

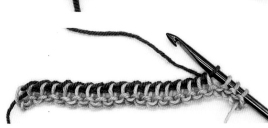

6. Turn fabric so that the front side is facing you and move the loops to the first hook. Being careful not to twist the foundation row, hold the 2 ends together.

7. Using the first end of the double-ended hook, insert the hook into the edge stitch as if it were a Tss.

8. Yarn over and pull up a loop.

9. Continue working the forward pass until all stitches are worked or the number of loops on the hook becomes uncomfortable. When this occurs, turn the fabric so the back side is facing you and continue working the Tunisian in the round return pass.

Finished piece
worked in the round

STRETCHY BIND-OFF

The stretchy bind-off is similar to the single crochet bind-off but with an added yarn under (yu) to give it an extra bit of stretch. This bind-off is great for lace projects that require vigorous blocking to open up the lace pattern.

1. Work the bind-off stitch indicated and pull a loop. Leave loop on hook and yarn under.

2. Pull yarn through all loops on hook.

How to Read a Pattern

Patterns in this book follow a standard format and use the same notations and abbreviations throughout. This section explains how to understand and work the patterns as intended.

DIFFICULTY LEVEL

Each pattern lists a difficulty level based on the stitches and techniques needed to complete the pattern. The patterns in this book start at level 1 and gradually increase in difficulty to level 4.

Level 1: Beginner patterns are suitable to all skill levels. These patterns use only basic stitches and minimal shaping.

Level 2: Easy patterns have limited stitches and stitch patterns along with easy shaping and color changes. These patterns feature easy-to-remember stitch patterns. Mistakes, such as a missed stitch, are quickly found or not critical.

Level 3: Intermediate patterns have more complicated stitch patterns, shaping, and techniques.

Level 4: Advanced patterns use a variety of stitches, can have intricate stitch patterns, and use advanced techniques and shaping.

YARN AND NOTIONS

The first part of any pattern lists the supplies you need to make the pattern exactly as shown.

Yarn

This will state the weight of the yarn (lace, fingering, sock, etc.), the fiber content of the yarn, and the amount you will need. If you are substituting yarn, you will want to make sure you're still able to get the gauge listed in the pattern.

Hook Size and Type

This will tell you the suggested hook size needed to get gauge. It will also tell you how long the hook and/or cable needs to be or if a double-ended hook is required. Tension and hook material can affect gauge, so it is important to swatch and adjust if necessary so the fabric has the correct consistency and the item is the correct size.

Notions

Notions are all the other items and tools that are needed to be able to create the pattern. This typically includes stitch markers, a tapestry needle, and technique-specific items such as a cable needle.

SWATCHING AND GAUGE

Everybody likes just jumping straight into the pattern. Why waste time on a gauge swatch? Is it always really needed? A gauge swatch can actually save you time by letting you know whether the yarn and hook chosen for the project will create the right fabric. Gauge can greatly influence the size of the project, so by swatching you ensure that the final project will fit as expected.

Gauge is defined for a specific stitch or stitch pattern. For designs like shawls, gauge is useful so that you know you're getting a fabric similar to the intended design. Getting close to the correct gauge is important, but getting the exact gauge is not critical. However, for designs that need to fit properly (hats, sweaters, socks), gauge is critical. If you're off by 1 stitch every 4 inches (10 cm), that could easily change the size of your garment so that it no longer fits.

How to Swatch for Gauge

Gauge is typically given in number of stitches and rows per 4 inches (10 cm). For an accurate measurement, create a swatch 5 inches (12.5 cm) or larger on all sides. Block the swatch exactly how you will block the finished object and allow the swatch to fully dry before measuring. When counting, use the middle of the swatch and do not include the edge stitches.

Row Gauge

Row gauge, the number of rows per 4 inches (10 cm), is determined by the forward pass and is mostly influenced by your hook. If you have more rows than needed in your gauge swatch, then you need to make your stitches taller. This can be done by using a larger hook size or possibly changing hook material to something more grippy, such as

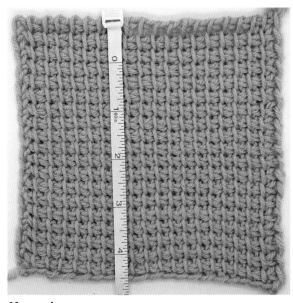

Measuring row gauge

bamboo. If you have fewer rows than needed in your gauge swatch, then you need to make your stitches shorter. This can be done using a smaller hook or changing to a smoother hook material, such as metal.

Stitch Gauge

Stitch gauge, the number of stitches per 4 inches (10 cm), is determined by the return pass and is influenced by a combination of the hook and your tension. If you have more stitches than needed, then your return pass is too tight. Adjust your hook size up or loosen up on the tension. If you don't have enough stitches in your gauge swatch, you need more tension on the return pass. Try a smaller hook.

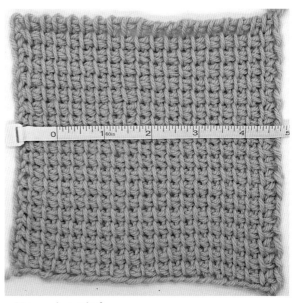

Measuring stitch gauge

FIT

As a factor in fit, ease is a measure of extra fabric compared to the body measurement. A loose-fitting top will have positive ease, whereas a very snug top or a hat will have negative ease so it fits close.

PATTERN NOTATIONS

- **Multiple stitches:** Tss 4 is shorthand for "work a Tss stitch in each of the next 4 stitches."
- **Brackets [ ]** indicate a group of stitches to be repeated. For example, "[Tss, Tks] 2 times" is the same as "Tss, Tks, Tss, Tks."
- **Asterisks *** are used to indicate a longer group of stitches to be repeated. In this example, "Row 8: Tss, Tks, *Tss, [Tks, Tss] 2 times, Tps 3; rep from * 15 times," the instructions between the first asterisk and the semicolon are repeated 15 times, while the 2 stitches before the * are worked only once.
- **Parentheses ( )** indicate that multiple stitches are to be worked into the next stitch. For example, "(Tss, Tks)" means "work a Tss in the next stitch, and then also work a Tks into the same stitch."
- **Repeat until:** When the pattern states "rep until 2 sts rem," that means the repeated portion of the forward pass should be continued until there are 2 sets of vertical bars left in the forward pass: the edge stitch and one set of vertical bars before that.
- **Stitch count:** In this book the stitch count is listed in italics at the end of the forward pass instructions. The stitch count for the row is the number of loops on the hook before the start of the return pass. This includes the first loop on the hook at the start of the row as well as any increases or decreases made during the forward pass. For example, "Row 3: Tss 3, Te. *5 sts*" means there are 5 loops on the hook: the first loop, 3 Tss stitches, and the Te stitch. The number of stitches is listed only when the total number of stitches in the row has changed.

BLOCKING

Blocking is the final step in all projects and is essential to even out the stitches, remove excess curl, and set the final size and shape of the finished piece. Some projects will need just a gentle blocking to even out the stitches and remove curl. Other projects, like lace, will need a vigorous blocking to open up the stitch pattern. This process is done by wetting the item when stitching is complete and allowing it to fully dry. There are three main methods of blocking.

Wet blocking is recommended for wool and other animal fibers. Place the item in a sink or bowl filled with water (follow the yarn label instructions for water temperature and soap). Submerge your project while gently squeezing out any air bubbles and then allow to soak until yarn is saturated.

Once the item has finished soaking, gently lift it out of the water bath and gently squeeze (do not wring) to remove excess water. Place the item between clean, dry towels and gently press to remove even more water.

Lay out your damp item on a flat surface. Gently pat it into the finished shape and size. Pin the item around the edges to hold the shape and allow to fully dry.

Steam blocking is recommended for acrylic yarn. While the item is dry, lay out and pin your project to finished shape and size. Hold the hand steamer or steam iron 1–2 inches (2.5–5 cm) above the item and allow the steam to permeate the yarn. Do not touch the fabric, as this can flatten the stitches. Allow item to fully dry before removing.

Spray blocking is recommended for delicate yarns or yarns that easily lose their shape while wet (such as cotton). The process for spray blocking is similar to steam blocking, but instead of using a hand steamer, spray the item with a combination of water and soap until the item is lightly saturated; allow to dry.

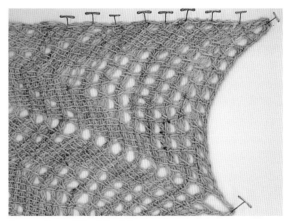

Lace pinned for blocking

PATTERN MODIFICATIONS

Many of the patterns have suggestions on how to modify the pattern to your liking. The yardage shown is for the default size. If you choose to make a larger-size project, have extra yarn available.

ABBREVIATIONS

CC	contrast color		**Tks**	Tunisian knit stitch
ch	chain		**Tmfs**	modified Tunisian full stitch
exTe	extended edge stitch		**Tmos**	Tunisian mosaic stitch
FP	forward pass		**Tmss**	modified Tunisian simple stitch
MC	main color		**Tps**	Tunisian purl stitch
MR	magic ring		**Trs**	Tunisian reverse stitch
pm	place stitch marker		**Tss**	Tunisian simple stitch
Ptrs	purled reverse stitch		**Tks2Tog**	Tks 2 stitches together
rem	remaining		**Trs2Tog**	Trs 2 stitches together
rep	repeat		**Tss2Tog**	Tss 2 stitches together
RP	return pass		**Tss3To**	Tss 3 stitches together
Rtks	reverse Tunisian knit stitch		**Ttop**	Tunisian top stitch
scBO	single crochet bind-off		**Twd**	twisted down simple stitch
slstBO	slip stitch bind-off		**Twks**	twisted knit stitch
sl st	slip stitch		**Twup**	twisted up simple stitch
sk	skip		**Tx**	Tunisian cross stitch
sk st	skip a stitch		**yo**	yarn over
st, sts	stitch, stitches		**yu**	yarn under
Tbss	back bar Tunisian simple stitch		**[ ]**	group of stitches to be repeated
Te	Tunisian edge stitch		*** ;**	larger group of stitches to be repeated
Tfs	Tunisian full stitch		**( )**	work all stitches in ( ) in next st

Patterns

Trailhead Cowl

This is a perfect first project on your Tunisian crochet journey. The Trailhead Cowl uses a regular crochet hook and the Tunisian simple stitch to create an easy and yet striking zigzag design. The cowl is extra warm on a chilly spring hike. The pattern calls for two colors, but feel free to experiment with more. Each section uses approximately 40 yards (36 m) of yarn.

YARN
Cascade 220 Superwash Merino (DK weight); 100% Superwash Merino; 220 yd (201 m) per 3.5 oz (100 g)

Colors:
MC: 18 Violet Tulip; 1 skein, 220 yd (201 m)
CC: 49 Hawaiian Ocean; 1 skein, 220 yd (201 m)

HOOK
6 mm (US J-10) crochet hook with at least a 2 in (5 cm) shaft

NOTIONS
Tapestry needle, removable stitch marker

GAUGE
16 Tss and 16 rows per 4 in (10 cm)

FINISHED SIZE
A: 9 in (22 cm)
B: 36 in (90 cm)

STITCHES AND TECHNIQUES
Tss, Te, Entrelac Join

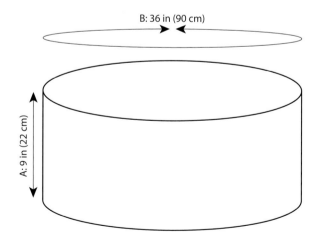

B: 36 in (90 cm)

A: 9 in (22 cm)

INSTRUCTIONS

Setup Chain: With MC, ch 60.
Note: *There are more chains than needed to make sure you have enough in case of miscounting. The extra chains should just be unraveled after Section 1 is complete.*

Section 1

Row 1: With MC, starting in the 2nd ch from hook, pick up a loop in the back bump of the next 7 ch. *8 sts.*
Row 1 RP and all RP until Row 25: Do not ch 1, [yo and pull through 2 loops] rep until 1 loop rem on hook.
Rows 2–6: Tss 6, pick up a loop in the next ch. *8 sts.*
Row 7: Tss 6, pick up a loop in the next 7 ch. *14 sts.*
Rows 8–11: Tss 12, pick up a loop in the next ch. *14 sts.*
Place removable stitch marker in the loop currently on hook (first repeat only; see photo 1).

Stitch marker placement

Row 12: Tss 12, pick up a loop in the next ch. *14 sts.*

Row 13: SlstBO 6, Tss 6, pick up a loop in the next 7 ch. *14 sts.*

Rows 14–19: Rep Rows 8–13 once.

Rows 20–24: Tss 12, pick up a loop in the next ch. *14 sts.*

Row 25: SlstBO 6, Tss 6, pick up a loop in the next 7 ch. *14 sts.*

Note: *After Row 25, stitches are no longer picked up in the starting chain.*

Row 25 RP and all remaining RP in Section 1: Work a standard RP.

Rows 26–30: Tss 12, Te. *14 sts.*

Row 31: SlstBO 6, Tss 6, Te. *8 sts.*

Rows 32–36: Tss 6, Te. *8 sts.*

Bind off: SlstBO across. Fasten off.

Section 2

Row 1: Join with CC and pick up 1 loop at marked st (photo 2). Remove marker. Pick up loop in the next 6 top sts (photo 3), pick up a loop in the next edge st (photo 4). *8 sts.*

Join at marked stitch.

Pick up 6 loops in top stitches.

Pick up loop in edge stitch.

Row 1 RP and all RP until Row 25: Work the RP as follows: Do not ch 1, [yo and pull through 2 loops] rep until 1 loop rem on hook.

Rows 2–6: Tss 6, pick up loop in next edge st. *8 sts.*

Row 7: Tss 6, pick up loop on the next 6 top sts, pick up a loop in the next edge st. *14 sts.*

Rows 8–11: Tss 12, pick up a loop in the next edge st. *14 sts.*

Place removable stitch marker on loop on hook (first repeat only).

Row 12: Tss 12, pick up a loop in the next edge st. *14 sts.*

Row 13: SlstBO 6, Tss 6, pick up a loop in the next 6 top sts, pick up a loop in the next edge st. *14 sts.*

Rows 14–19: Rep Rows 8–13 once.

Rows 20–24: Tss 12, pick up a loop in the next edge st. *14 sts.*

Row 25: SlstBO 6, Tss 6, pick up a loop in the next 6 top sts, Te. *14 sts.*

Row 25 RP and all remaining RP in section 2: Work a standard RP.

Rows 26–30: Tss 12, Te. *14 sts.*

Row 31: SlstBO 6, Tss 6, Te. *8 sts.*

Rows 32–36: Tss 6, Te. *8 sts.*

Bind off: SlstBO across. Fasten off.

Rep Section 2, alternating between MC and CC.

For a 36 in (90 cm) circumference cowl, repeat section 2 an additional 10 times for a total of 11 repeats. Additional repeats can be added for a longer cowl.

Finishing

Weave in ends. Sew the first and last sections together by laying the two ends next to each other so they form a solid fabric and sewing along blocks. Wet block gently to remove curl without stretching out the cowl.

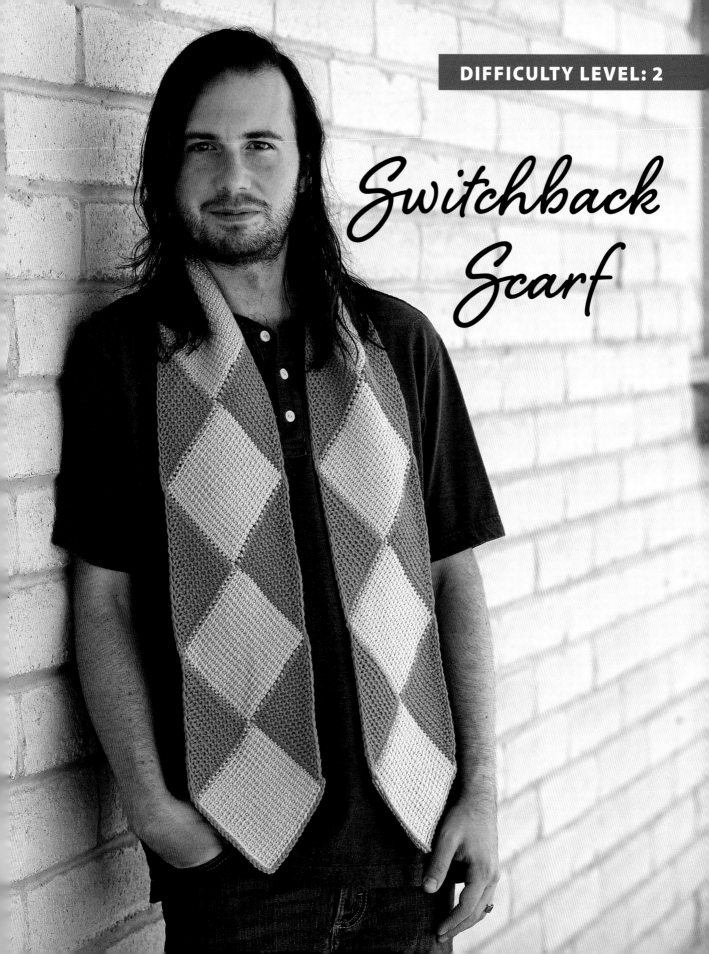

Switchback Scarf

The versatile Switchback Scarf, with big bold squares and a triangle border, puts a new twist on classic entrelac. This easy scarf can be made with a 6-in (15-cm) straight crochet hook or a Tunisian crochet hook. This scarf is an eye-catching accessory year-round, whether looking for neck warmth or a fashionably light accent. The squares are worked first, one at a time. When all the squares are completed, the triangle border is worked around the squares. This scarf uses the modified Tunisian simple stitch for the squares and the Tunisian purl stitch with easy shaping for the triangle border.

YARN
Cascade 220 Superwash Merino (DK weight); 100% Superwash Merino; 220 yd (201 m) per 3.5 oz (100 g)

Colors:
MC: 64 Glacier Grey; 1 skein, 220 yd (201 m)
CC: 49 Hawaiian Ocean; 1 skein, 220 yd (201 m)

HOOK
6 mm (US J-10) Tunisian crochet hook at least 6 in (15 cm) long

NOTIONS
Tapestry needle, removable stitch marker

GAUGE
16 Tmss and 16 rows per 4 in (10 cm)

FINISHED SIZE
A: 60 in (150 cm)
B: 6 in (15 cm)

STITCHES AND TECHNIQUES
Tmss, Tps, Entrelac Join

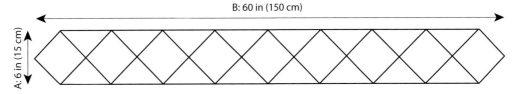

B: 60 in (150 cm)

A: 6 in (15 cm)

INSTRUCTIONS

Setup Chain: With MC, ch 333.
*Note: There are more chains than needed to ensure
there are enough chains in case of miscounting.
The extra chains should be unraveled after
completion of Section 1.*

Section 1: Squares

SQUARE 1

Row 1: Starting in the 2nd ch from hook, pick up a
loop in the back bump of the next 19 ch. *20 sts.*
Row 1 RP and all RP in Section 1: Work the RP
as follows: Do not ch 1, [yo and pull through 2
loops] rep until 1 loop rem on hook.
Rows 2–17: Tmss 17, Tss, pick up a loop in the next
ch. *20 sts.*
Bind off: Place removable stitch marker in the loop
currently on hook (photo 1). Then [work each
st as Tmss and then sl st through loop on hook]

18 times, pick up a loop in the next ch and sl st
through loop on hook. *1 loop on hook.*

Stitch marker placement

SQUARE 2

Row 1: Pick up a loop in the next 19 ch. *20 sts.*
Rows 2–17: Tmss 17, Tss, pick up a loop in the next
ch. *20 sts.*
Bind off: [Work each st as Tmss and then sl st
through loop on hook] 18 times, pick up a loop
in the next ch and sl st through loop on hook. *1
loop on hook.*

SQUARES 3–9

Rep Square 2.
Fasten off at the end of the last square. Unravel any extra ch sts.

Section 2: Triangle Border

TRIANGLE 1

Row 1: With CC, join with sl st at the marked st, and then pick up a loop in each of the next 17 sts (photo 2). Skip 1 st and entrelac join to the edge st. *19 sts.*

Pick up stitches.

Row 1 RP and all Section 2 RP unless stated otherwise: Work the RP as follows: Do not ch 1, [yo and pull through 2 loops] rep until 3 loops rem on hook, yo and pull through 3 loops.

Note: *There is a decrease at the end of the RP for this section. In the next FP, skip both sets of vertical bars that were decreased together at the beginning of the row.*

Row 2: Tps 16, entrelac join. *18 sts.*
Row 3: Tps 15, entrelac join. *17 sts.*
Row 4: Tps 14, entrelac join. *16 sts.*
Rows 5–16: Tps across, entrelac join.
Row 17: Tps, entrelac join. *3 sts.*
Row 17 RP: Yo and pull through all loops.
Pick up a loop in the next st and sl st through loop on hook. *1 loop on hook.*

TRIANGLE 2

Row 1: Pick up a loop in the next 17 sts. Skip 1 st and entrelac join to the edge st. *19 sts.*
Row 2: Tps 16, entrelac join. *18 sts.*
Row 3: Tps 15, entrelac join. *17 sts.*
Row 4: Tps 14, entrelac join. *16 sts.*
Rows 5–16: Tps across, entrelac join.
Row 17: Tps, entrelac join. *3 sts.*

Row 17 RP: Yo and pull through all loops.
Pick up a loop in the next st and sl st through loop
on hook. *1 loop on hook.*

TRIANGLES 3–8

Rep Triangle 2.
Sl st in back loop of the next 18 ch (photos 3 and 4).
Turn to continue working along the edge of the
square and sl st in the back loop of the next 19
ch (photos 5 and 6).

Work second side of square.

Insert hook into back loop.

Work a slip stitch.

Turn work.

TRIANGLES 9–16

Rep Triangle 2 an additional 8 times. Sl st in the
back loop of the next 19 ch. Turn to continue
working along the edge of the square and sl st
in the back loop of the next 18 ch. Sl st in the
Triangle 1 join.

Finishing

Fasten off and weave in ends. Block gently to
remove curl.

DIFFICULTY LEVEL: 2

Ridgeline Scarf

Time to further expand your stitch repertoire. This snuggly scarf is loaded with raised diagonal ridges flowing down the length of the scarf and is perfect for wrapping up and staying warm during chilly winter months. The Ridgeline Scarf is worked on the bias using Trs, Tps, and Ptrs to create ridges of varying textures. The length and width of this scarf can easily be modified to accommodate the maker's preference.

YARN
Cascade 220 Superwash Aran (Aran weight); 100% Superwash Merino; 150 yd (137.2 m) per 3.5 oz (100 g)

Color: 248 Flint Stone; 2 skeins, 300 yd (274.3 m)

HOOK
8 mm (US L-11) Tunisian crochet hook at least 6 in (15 cm) long

NOTIONS
Tapestry needle, removable stitch marker

GAUGE
12 Tks and 16 rows per 4 in (10 cm)

FINISHED SIZE
A: 6 in (15 cm)
B: 55 in (140 cm)

STITCHES AND TECHNIQUES
Tks, Trs, Tps, Ptrs, Te, exTe

MODIFICATIONS
The scarf width can be increased by 1 in (2.5 cm) by adding 5 extra chains to the foundation row chain.

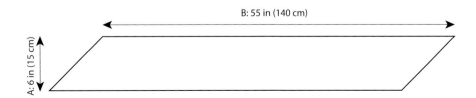

B: 55 in (140 cm)

A: 6 in (15 cm)

INSTRUCTIONS

Foundation Row: Ch 30. Starting in the 2nd ch from hook, pick up a loop in the back bump of all chains. *30 sts.*

Foundation Row RP: Work a standard RP.

Note: *The bias is created by an increase at the end of each forward pass and a decrease at the end of each return pass. The increase at the end of the forward pass is created by first working exTe and then a Te into the edge stitch.*

It can be helpful to use a removable stitch marker to mark the first Tks row of a set (i.e., Rows 2, 8, 14).

Row 1: Ptrs 28, (exTe, Te). *31 sts.*

Note: *The ( ) indicates multiple stitches to be worked in 1 space. On all rows, work an exTe and a Te into the last st.*

Row 1 RP and all following RP: Work the RP as follows: Ch 1, [yo and pull through 2 loops] rep until 3 loops rem on hook (photo 1), yo and pull through 3 loops (photo 2). *1 st decreased.*

Note: *There is a decrease at the end of the RP. In the next FP, skip both sets of vertical bars that were decreased together at the beginning of the row (photo 3).*

Return Pass: 3 loops rem on hook.

After yarn over and pull through 3 loops, 1 loop on hook.

Start with third set of vertical bars.

Rows 2–6: Tks 28, (exTe, Te).
Row 7: Trs 28, (exTe, Te).
Rows 8–12: Tks 28 (exTe, Te).
Row 13: Ptrs 28, (exTe, Te).
Rows 14–18: Tks 28, (exTe, Te).
Row 19: Tps 28, (exTe, Te).
Row 20: Ptrs 28, (exTe, Te).
Rows 21–25: Tks 28, (exTe, Te).
Row 26: Ptrs 28, (exTe, Te).
Rows 27–31: Tks 28, (exTe, Te).
Row 32: Trs 28, (exTe, Te).
Rows 33–107: Rep Rows 8–32 3 more times or until desired length.
Rows 108–112: Tks 28, (exTe, Te).
Bind off: [Work each st as Ptrs and then sl st through loop on hook] to end. *1 loop on hook.*

Finishing

Fasten off and weave in ends. Block gently to remove curl, being careful not to flatten the ridges.

Waterfall Shawl

O ur first shawl pattern utilizes a classy but easy eyelet design to create the effect of multiple waterfalls flowing down this shallow triangle shawl. The Waterfall Shawl is worked sideways from point to point. This makes for a fun, lightweight shawl, which can easily be modified for any amount of yarn. When working the shawl, Section 1 increases to the maximum width, at which point half the yarn will be used. Section 2 decreases back down to a point.

YARN

Cascade Heritage Silk (Fingering weight); 85% Superwash Merino, 15% silk; 437 yd (399.6 m) per 3.5 oz (100 g)

Color: 5732 Delphinium; 2 skeins, 600 yd (548.6 m)

HOOK

5.5 mm (US I-9) Tunisian crochet hook with cable at least 12 in (40 cm) long

NOTIONS

Tapestry needle

GAUGE

20 Tss and 20 rows per 4 in (10 cm)

FINISHED SIZE

A: 20 in (50 cm)
B: 75 in (190 cm)

STITCHES AND TECHNIQUES

MR, Tss, Tks, Tss2Tog, Te, exTe

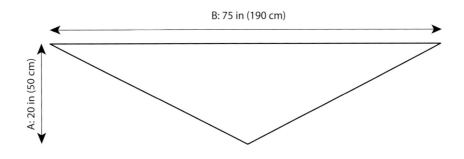

INSTRUCTIONS

Foundation Row: [Insert hook into MR, yo and pull up a loop, ch 1] 3 times. *3 sts.*

Foundation Row RP and all following RP: Work a standard RP.

Section 1

Row 1: Tss, (exTe, Te). *4 sts.*

Note: *The ( ) indicates multiple stitches to be worked in 1 space. On Row 1, work an exTe and a Te into the last st (see photos 1 and 2).*

ExTe

ExTe and Te in edge stitch

Row 2: Tss 2, Te. *4 sts.*
Row 3: Tss 2, (exTe, Te). *5 sts.*
Row 4: Tss 3, Te. *5 sts.*
Row 5: Tss 3, (exTe, Te). *6 sts.*
Row 6: Tss to last st, Te. *6 sts.*

Row 7: Tss to last st, (exTe, Te). *7 sts.*
Rows 8–37: Rep Rows 6–7.
Note: *When doing a double yarn over (yo 2), treat them as 2 stitches in the return pass.*
Row 38: [Tss, Tss2Tog, yo 2, Tss2Tog, Tss 5] rep to last st, Te. *22 sts.* (See photos 3, 4, and 5.)

Double yarn over

Tss2Tog after double yarn over

Double yarn over after return pass

Note: *In the following row, both a Tks and a Tss (bolded) will be worked into the double yarn over (see photos 6, 7, and 8).*

Row 39: [Tss2Tog, yo, **Tks**, **Tss**, yo, Tss2Tog, Tss 4] rep to last st, (exTe, Te). *23 sts.*

Tks in double yarn over

Tss location in double yarn over

Tks and Tss in double yarn over

Row 40: Tss, [Tks, Tss 2, Tks, yo, Tss2Tog, Tss 2, Tss2Tog, yo] rep to last st, Te. *23 sts.*

Row 41: Tss, [Tss 4, Tks, yo, Tss2Tog 2, yo, Tks] rep to last st, (exTe, Te). *24 sts.*

Row 42: Tss 2, [Tss 4, Tks, yo 2, sk 2, Tks, Tss 2] rep to last st, Te. *24 sts.*

Row 43: Tss 2, [Tss 5, Tks, Tss 4] rep to last st, (exTe, Te). *25 sts.*

Rows 44–123: Rep Rows 24–43 4 more times. For a larger shawl, work more repeats before continuing to Row 124. You will also need to work the same number of additional repeats in Section 2, Rows 138–157. Each repeat adds another 10 sts.

Rows 124–129: Rep Rows 6–7 3 times.

Rows 130–131: Tss to last st, Te. *+0 sts/row.*

Section 2

Row 132: Tss to last st, Te. *+0 sts/row.*

Row 133: Tss until 2 sts rem, Tss2Tog. *–1 st/row.*

Note: *Tss2Tog at end of forward pass is in the last Tss and the Te.*

Rows 134–137: Rep Rows 132–133.

Row 138: Tss 3, [Tss 3, Tss2Tog, yo 2, Tss2Tog, Tss 3] rep to last st, Te.

Row 139: Tss 2, [Tss 3, Tss2Tog, yo, Tks, Tss, yo, Tss2Tog, Tss] rep until 2 sts rem, Tss2Tog.

Row 140: Tss 2, [Tss 2, Tss2Tog, yo, Tks, Tss 2, Tks, yo, Tss2Tog] rep to last st, Te.

Row 141: Tss, [yo, Tss2Tog 2, yo, Tks, Tss 4, Tks] rep until 2 sts rem, Tss2Tog.

Row 142: Tss, [Tks, yo 2, sk 2, Tks, Tss 6] rep to last st, Te.

Row 143: [Tss 2, Tks, Tss 7] rep until 2 sts rem, Tss2Tog.

Rows 144–157: Rep Rows 132–133.

Rows 158–237: Rep Rows 138–157 4 more times, or, for a larger shawl, work more repeats as you did in Section 1.

Rows 238–261: Rep Rows 132–133.

Row 262: Tss, Te, yo and pull through all loops.

Finishing

Fasten off and weave in ends. Block enthusiastically to open up the eyelets.

Daytrip Cowl

The Daytrip Cowl is a quick, fun cowl using Tunisian full stitch. Made with Aran weight yarn, this cowl can easily be completed in a single day. It is worked flat from the bottom and then sewn. This cowl introduces changing colors to create stripes.

YARN
Cascade 220 Superwash Aran (Aran weight); 100% Superwash Merino; 150 yd (137 m) per 3.5 oz (100 g)

Colors:
MC: 1993 Smoke Blue; 1 skein, 120 yd (110 m)
CC: 1989 Royal Purple; 1 skein, 75 yd (69 m)

HOOK
8 mm (US L-11) Tunisian crochet hook with cable at least 16 in (40 cm) long

NOTIONS
Tapestry needle

GAUGE
10 Tfs and 14 rows per 4 in (10 cm)

FINISHED SIZE
A: 9 in (20 cm)
B: 28 in (70 cm)

STITCHES AND TECHNIQUES
Tfs, Te

Return pass with color change (RPCC): Ch 1, [yo and pull through 2 loops] rep until 2 loops rem on hook, drop current color, pick up next color, yo and pull through 2 loops.

Tunisian full stitch (Tfs): Tunisian full stitch is worked in the space between 2 sets of vertical bars. The space into which the first stitch of the row is worked alternates between the first space and the second space. In odd-numbered rows, the first Tfs is worked into the first space and there is no stitch worked into the space immediately before the edge stitch (photos 1 and 2). In even-numbered rows, skip the first space and work the first Tfs into the second space (photos 3 and 4), and then work the last Tfs into the space immediately before the edge stitch.

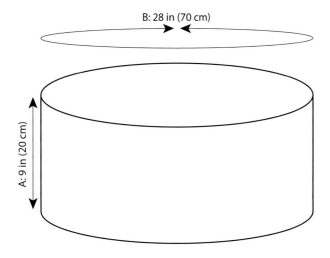

B: 28 in (70 cm)

A: 9 in (20 cm)

Odd row

First Tfs worked before second set of vertical bars

Even row

First Tfs worked after second set of vertical bars

INSTRUCTIONS

Foundation Row: With CC, ch 74. Starting in the 2nd ch from hook, pick up a loop in the back bump of all chains. *74 sts*

Foundation Row RP and all following RP unless stated otherwise: Work a standard RP.

Row 1: With CC, Tfs before the second set of vertical bars, Tfs 71, sk st, Te. RPCC.

Row 2: With MC, Tfs between the second and third set of vertical bars, Tfs 71, Te.

Row 3: With MC, Tfs before the second set of vertical bars, Tfs 71, sk st, Te.

Row 4: With MC, Tfs between the second and third set of vertical bars, Tfs 71, Te.

Row 5: With MC, Tfs before the second set of vertical bars, Tfs 71, sk next st, Te. RPCC.

Row 6: With CC, Tfs between the second and third set of vertical bars, Tfs 71, Te.

Row 7: With CC, Tfs before the second set of vertical bars, Tfs 71, sk next st, Te. RPCC.

Rows 8–25: Rep Rows 2–7 an additional 3 times for a total of 4 repeats.

Rows 26–30: Rep Rows 2–6 once.

Bind off: [Work each st as Tfs and pull up a loop. Yo and pull through both loops on hook] to end. *1 loop on hook.*

Finishing

Fasten off and weave in ends. Lay ends next to each other and sew together. Block gently to reduce curl.

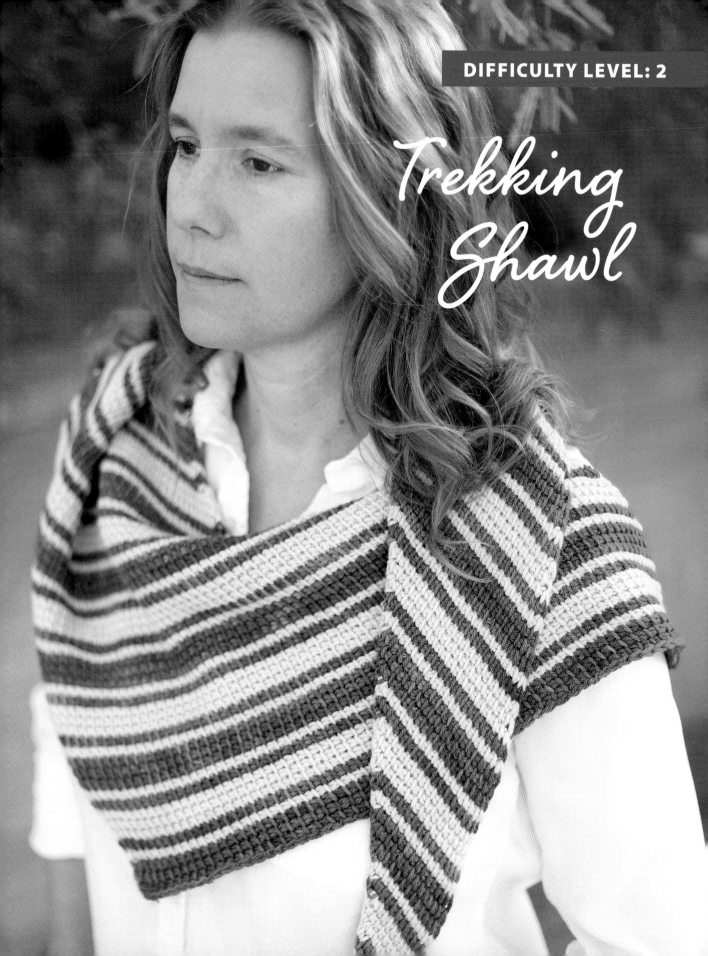

Trekking
Shawl

The Trekking Shawl's stripes and easy boomerang shaping make for a relaxing and enjoyable project. The asymmetric nature of the shaping allows the shawl to drape nicely around the shoulders, so it can be thrown on quickly to dress up any outfit when running out the door. The shape is created by an increase at the end of every forward pass and a decrease at the end of every other return pass. The design uses equal amounts of two colors. While the sample is worked in DK weight yarn, any weight from fingering to worsted will work, and the length can be adjusted to accommodate the maker's preference.

YARN
Seismic Yarn Butter Sock DK (DK weight); 85% Superwash Merino, 15% nylon; 246 yd (225 m) per 3.5 oz (100 g)

Colors:
MC: Azurite & Malachite; 1 skein, 246 yd (225 m)
CC: Aquatic Pearl; 1 skein, 246 yd (225 m)

HOOK
6.5 mm (US K-10.5) Tunisian crochet hook with cable at least 12 in (30 cm) long

NOTIONS
Tapestry needle, removable stitch marker

GAUGE
16 Tss and 16 rows per 4 in (10 cm)

FINISHED SIZE
A: 14 in (35 cm)
B: 70 in (180 cm)

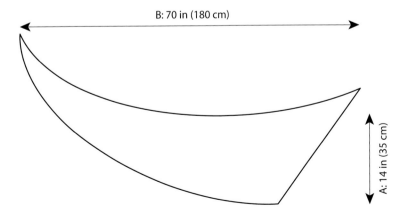

B: 70 in (180 cm)

A: 14 in (35 cm)

STITCHES AND TECHNIQUES
Tss, Te, exTe

Return pass with decrease (RPD): Ch 1, [yo and pull through 2 loops] rep until 3 loops rem on hook, yo and pull through 3 loops. *1 st decreased.*

Return pass with decrease with color change (RPD-CC): Ch 1, [yo and pull through 2 loops] rep until 3 loops rem on hook, drop current color, pick up next color, yo and pull through all loops. *1 st decreased.*

Note: *For return passes with decreases, the 2 loops decreased together at end of RP are treated like 1 st in the next row and not worked.*

Return pass with color change (RPCC): Ch 1, [yo and pull through 2 loops] rep until 2 loops rem on hook, drop current color, pick up next color, yo and pull through all loops.

INSTRUCTIONS

Foundation Row: With MC, ch 3. Starting in the 2nd ch from hook, pick up a loop in the back bump of all chains. *3 sts.*

Foundation Row RP: For this and all following RP unless stated otherwise, work a standard RP.

Row 1: Tss, (exTe, Te). *4 sts.*

Note: *The ( ) indicates multiple stitches to be worked in 1 space. In all rows, work an exTe and then a Te into the last st.*

Row 2: Tss 2, (exTe, Te). *5 sts.* RPD.

Row 3: Tss 2, (exTe, Te). *5 sts.* RPCC.

Row 4: With CC, Tss 3, (exTe, Te). *6 sts.* RPD-CC.

Row 5: With MC, Tss 3, (exTe, Te). *6 sts.* RPCC.

Row 6: With CC, Tss to last st, (exTe, Te). *+1 st.* RPD.

Row 7: Tss to last st, (exTe, Te). *+0 sts.*

Row 8: Tss to last st, (exTe, Te). *+1 st.* RPD-CC.

Row 9: With MC, Tss to last st, (exTe, Te). *+0 sts.* RPCC.

Row 10: With CC, Tss to last st, (exTe, Te). +1 st. RPD-CC.
Row 11: With MC, Tss to last st, (exTe, Te). +0 sts.
Row 12: Tss to last st, (exTe, Te). +1 st. RPD.
Row 13: Tss to last st, (exTe, Te). +0 sts. RPCC.

Row 14: With CC, Tss to last st, (exTe, Te). +1 st. RPD-CC.
Row 15: With MC, Tss to last st, (exTe, Te). +0 sts. RPCC.
Rep Rows 6–15 an additional 13 times or until desired size.
Row 16: With CC, Tss to last st, (exTe, Te). +1 st. RPD.
Row 17: Tss to last st, (exTe, Te). +0 sts.
Row 18: Tss to last st, (exTe, Te). +1 st. RPD.
Bind off: SlstBO in Tss all sts.

Finishing

Fasten off and weave in ends. Block gently to remove curl.

Water's Edge Shawl

re you ready to dip your toes into short rows? Inspired by ripples on a still body of water, the Water's Edge Shawl uses a technique called short rows to fade between three colors and create a long, shallow, crescent-shaped shawl. Short rows may sound complicated, but they are simply a row in which some of the stitches are left unworked. This handy technique is often used to create interesting and unique shaping.

YARN
Marianated Yarns Playtime DK (DK weight); 100% Superwash Merino; 274 yd (251 m) per 3.5 oz (100 g)

Colors:
C1: Glacial Lake; 1 skein, 200 yd (183 m)
C2: Sea of Glass; 1 skein, 274 yd (251 m)
C3: Tidal Pool; 1 skein, 274 yd (251 m)

HOOK
6 mm (US J-10) Tunisian crochet hook with cable at least 16 in (40 cm) long

NOTIONS
Tapestry needle, removable stitch marker

GAUGE
14 Tss and 14 rows per 4 in (10 cm)

FINISHED SIZE
A: 14 in (35 cm)
B: 75 in (190 cm)

STITCHES AND TECHNIQUES
MR, Tss, Tks, Te

Return pass with color change (RPCC): Ch 1, [yo and pull through 2 loops] rep until 2 loops rem on hook, drop current color, pick up next color, yo and pull through 2 loops.

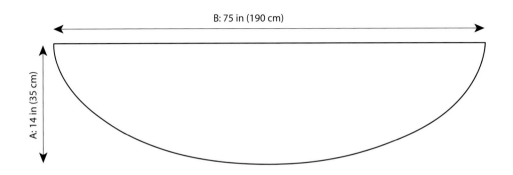

B: 75 in (190 cm)

A: 14 in (35 cm)

INSTRUCTIONS

Foundation Row: With C1, [insert hook into MR, pull up a loop, ch 1] 3 times. *3 sts.*

Foundation Row RP and all following RP unless stated otherwise: Work a standard RP.

Row 1: Yo, (Tks, yo, Tks), yo, Te. *7 sts.*

Note: *The ( ) indicates multiple stitches to be worked in 1 space. For (Tks, yo, Tks), work a Tks in the next st, yo, and then work a second Tks in the same st.*

Row 2: Tss, yo, (Tks, Tss), Tss, (Tks, Tss), yo, Tss, Te. *11 sts.*

Row 3: Tss, yo, (Tks, Tss), Tss 5, (Tks, Tss), yo, Tss, Te. *15 sts.*

Note: *The (Tks, Tss) at the beginning and end of the forward pass are worked into the yo of the previous row. The Tks is worked into the large open space created by the yo (photo 1). The Tss is worked behind the front vertical bar (photo 2).*

Tks in yarn over

Tss in yarn over

Row 4: Tss, yo, (Tks, Tss), Tss 9, (Tks, Tss), yo, Tss, Te. *19 sts.*

Row 5: Tss, yo, (Tks, Tss), Tss 13, (Tks, Tss), yo, Tss, Te. *23 sts.*

Rows 6–29: Tss, yo, (Tks, Tss), Tss until 3 sts rem, (Tks, Tss), yo, Tss, Te. *+4 sts/row.*

Row 30: Tss, yo, (Tks, Tss), Tss until 3 sts rem, (Tks, Tss), yo, Tss, Te. *123 sts.* RPCC.

Row 31: With C2, Tss, yo, (Tks, Tss), Tss until 3 sts rem, (Tks, Tss), yo, Tss, Te. *127 sts.* RPCC.

Note: *Rows 32–50 are short rows. Leave the rest of the row unworked. Move the stitch marker to the last loop on hook before working the RP (photos 3 and 4).*

Stitch marker moved to last stitch

Return pass for short row

Row 32: With C1, Tss, yo, (Tks, Tss), Tss 6. Place stitch marker in last Tss. *11 sts.* RPCC.

Row 33: With C2, Tss, yo, (Tks, Tss), Tss to marked st, Tss in marked st, Tss 6, and move marker. *19 sts.* RPCC.

Row 34: With C1, Tss, yo, (Tks, Tss), Tss to marked st, Tss in marked st, Tss 6, and move marker. *27 sts.* RPCC.

Rows 35–50: Rep Rows 33–34. *+8 sts/row.* Fasten off C1.

Row 51: With C2, Tss, yo, (Tks, Tss), Tss until 3 sts rem, (Tks, Tss), yo, Tss, Te. *169 sts.*

Row 52: Tss, yo, (Tks, Tss), Tss 8. Place stitch marker in last Tss. *13 sts.*

Rows 53–70: Tss, yo, (Tks, Tss), Tss to marked st, Tss in marked st, Tss 8, and move marker. *+10 sts/row.*

Row 71: Tss, yo, (Tks, Tss), Tss to marked st, Tss in marked st, Tss 8, and move marker. *203 sts.* RPCC.

Row 72: With C3, Tss, yo, (Tks, Tss), Tss until 3 sts rem, (Tks, Tss), yo, Tss, Te. *213 sts.* RPCC.

Row 73: With C2, Tss, yo, (Tks, Tss), Tss 175. *180 sts.* RPCC.

Note: *For Rows 74 and all remaining even rows, the full row is worked.*

Row 74: Rep Row 72. *219 sts.*

Row 75: With C2, Tss, yo, (Tks, Tss), Tss 144. *149 sts.* RPCC.

Row 76: Rep Row 72. *225 sts.*

Row 77: With C2, Tss, yo, (Tks, Tss), Tss 113. *118 sts.* RPCC.

Row 78: Rep Row 72. *231 sts.*

Row 79: With C2, Tss, yo, (Tks, Tss), Tss 82. *87 sts.* RPCC.

Row 80: Rep Row 72. *237 sts.*

Row 81: With C2, Tss, yo, (Tks, Tss), Tss 51. *56 sts.* RPCC. Fasten off C2.

Rows 82–91: Rep Row 72. *243 sts.*

Bind off: ScBO in Tss.

Finishing

Fasten off and weave in ends. Block gently to remove curl.

Wild Berries Shawl

W ith its stunning deep-red color and lace bands, the Wild Berries Shawl evokes memories of enjoying a slice of lattice-crusted berry pie on a warm summer evening. This intermediate-level shawl starts by establishing the crescent shaping in Tunisian simple stitch. Alternating bands of lace and solid fabric create a sophisticated summer accessory. For this design, you'll use the stretchy bind-off for the first time, which allows the lace bands to fully open up with blocking.

YARN
MadelineTosh Tosh DK (DK weight); 100% Superwash Merino; 225 yd (206 m) per 4 oz (113 g)

Color: Siren; 3 skeins, 675 yd (617 m)

HOOK
6.5 mm (US K-10.5) Tunisian crochet hook with cable at least 16 in (40 cm) long

NOTIONS
Tapestry needle, removable stitch marker

GAUGE
14 Tss and 14 rows per 4 in (10 cm)

Getting a good drape is more important than getting the right gauge. The Tss portion of the fabric should be solid but not dense.

FINISHED SIZE
A: 20 in (50 cm)
B: 75 in (190 cm)

STITCHES AND TECHNIQUES
MR, Tss, Tss2Tog, Tks, Rtks, Trs, Trs2Tog, Tps, Te

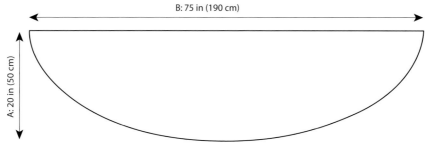

B: 75 in (190 cm)

A: 20 in (50 cm)

INSTRUCTIONS

Foundation Row: [Insert hook into MR, pull up a loop, ch 1] 4 times. *4 sts.*

Foundation Row RP and all following RP: Work a standard RP.

Row 1: (Tks, Tss, Tks) 2 times, Te. *8 sts.*

Note: *The ( ) indicates multiple stitches to be worked in 1 space. In this instance, work a Tks, then a Tss, and then another Tks into 1 st space.*

Row 2: Tss, (Tks, Tss, Tks), Tss 2, (Tks, Tss, Tks), Tss, Te. *12 sts.*

Row 3: Tss, (Tks, Tss, Tks), Tss 6, (Tks, Tss, Tks), Tss, Te. *16 sts.*

Row 4: Tss, (Tks, Tss, Tks), Tss 10, (Tks, Tss, Tks), Tss, Te. *20 sts.*

Row 5: Tss, (Tks, Tss, Tks), Tss 14, (Tks, Tss, Tks), Tss, Te. *24 sts.*

Row 6: Tss, (Tks, Tss, Tks), Tss until 3 sts rem, (Tks, Tss, Tks), Tss, Te. *28 sts.*

Rows 7–16: Rep Row 6. *+4 sts/row.*

Row 17: Tss, (Tks, Tss, Tks), [Trs2Tog, yo] rep until 3 sts rem, (Tks, Tss, Tks), Tss, Te. *72 sts.*

Note: *If you get to the end of forward pass and find you have an even number of sts left, don't worry about finding where the mistake occurred; just substitute a Trs for the last Trs2Tog, and the rest of the lace band will work just fine.*

Row 18: Tss, (Tks, Tss, Tks), yo, Tss2Tog, [yo, sk st, Tks] rep until 5 sts rem, yo, Tss2Tog, (Tks, Tss, Tks), Tss, Te. *76 sts.*

Note: *The Tks in [yo, sk st, Tks] should always be going into a yo on the previous row.*

Row 19: Tss, (Tks, Tss, Tks), Tss2Tog, yo, [Tks, yo, sk st] rep until 5 sts rem, Tss2Tog, yo, (Tks, Tss, Tks), Tss, Te. *80 sts.*

Row 20: Tss, (Tks, Tss, Tks), Trs 3, [Rtks, Tps] rep until 4 sts rem, Trs, (Tks, Tss, Tks), Tss, Te. *84 sts.*

Rows 21–36: Rep Row 6. *148 sts.*

Rows 37–39: Rep Rows 17–19. *160 sts.*

Rows 40–42: Rep Rows 18–20. *172 sts.*

Rows 43–58: Rep Row 6. *236 sts.*

Rows 59–61: Rep Rows 17–19. *248 sts.*

Rows 62–65: Rep Rows 18–19 twice. *264 sts.*
Bind off: Using the stretchy bind-off, work as
  follows: Tss 5, [Tks, Tss] rep until 4 sts rem, Tss 3,
  Te.

Finishing
Fasten off and weave in all ends. Block vigorously
to open up the lace panels.

Wanderlust Scarf

The Wanderlust Scarf uses Tunisian mosaic stitch to create a fun colorwork scarf perfect for outdoor adventuring. The Tunisian mosaic stitch is worked one row below normal to create this stunning colorwork. The scarf starts at a point and increases on both sides of the forward pass until it reaches the maximum width. At the end of the scarf, the return pass is used to decrease the scarf back to a point.

YARN
Cascade 220 Merino (Worsted weight); 100% merino; 220 yd (201 m) per 3.5 oz (100 g)

Colors:
MC: 67 Crushed Grape; 1 skein, 220 yd (201 m)
CC: 11 Pewter; 1 skein, 220 yd (201 m)

HOOK
6 mm (US J-10) Tunisian crochet hook at least 6 in (15 cm) long

NOTIONS
Tapestry needle, removable stitch marker

GAUGE
14 Tss and 14 rows per 4 in (10 cm)

FINISHED SIZE
A: 7 in (18 cm)
B: 60 in (150 cm)

STITCHES AND TECHNIQUES
MR, Tss, Tmss, Tmos, Ttop, Te

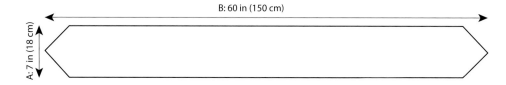

B: 60 in (150 cm)

A: 7 in (18 cm)

Tunisian mosaic stitch (Tmos): Tunisian mosaic stitch is worked 1 row below the current row. Insert the hook behind the vertical bar and under the top horizontal bar (photo 1). Yo and pull up a loop (photo 2) and then ch 1 (photo 3). The ch 1 is required to keep the fabric from excessively curling.

Insert hook behind front vertical bar and top horizontal bar.

Yarn over and pull up a loop.

Chain 1.

Return pass with color change (RPCC): Ch 1, [yo and pull through 2 loops] rep until 2 loops rem on hook, drop current color, pick up next color. Yo and pull through 2 loops.

Return pass with decrease and color change (RPD-CC): Do not ch 1, [yo and pull through 2 loops] rep until 3 loops rem on hook, drop current color, pick up next color, yo and pull through 3 loops. *2 sts decreased.*

Note: *Treat the 2 stitches decreased together at the beginning and end of the return pass as 1 st each in the next forward pass.*

INSTRUCTIONS

Foundation Row: [Insert hook into MR, pull up a loop, ch 1] 3 times. *3 sts.*

Foundation Row RP: Work a standard RP.

Increase Section

Row 1: With MC, Ttop, Tss, Ttop, Te. *5 sts.* RPCC.

Row 2: With CC, (Tss, Tmss), Tss, (Tmss, Tss), Te. *7 sts.* RPCC.

Note: *The ( ) indicates multiple stitches to be worked in 1 space. In Row 2, work a Tss and then a Tmss into the first st.*

Row 3: With MC, (Tss, Tmss), Tmos, Tss 3, Ttop, Te. *9 sts.* RPCC.

Row 4: With CC, (Tss, Tmss), Tmos, Tss 5, Ttop, Te. *11 sts.* RPCC.

Row 5: With MC, (Tss, Tmss), Tss 6, Tmos, Tss, Ttop, Te. *13 sts.* RPCC.

Row 6: With CC, (Tss, Tmss), Tss 8, Tmos, Tss, Ttop, Te. *15 sts.* RPCC.

Row 7: With MC, (Tss, Tmss), Tmos, Tss 11, Ttop, Te. *17 sts.* RPCC.

Row 8: With CC, (Tss, Tmss), Tmos, Tss 13, Ttop, Te. *19 sts.* RPCC.

Row 9: With MC, (Tss, Tmss), Tmos, Tss 13, Tmos, Tss, Ttop, Te. *21 sts.* RPCC.

Row 10: With CC, (Tss, Tmss), Tmos, Tss, Tmos, Tss 13, Tmos, Tss, Ttop, Te. *23 sts.* RPCC.

Row 11: With MC, (Tss, Tmss), [Tmos, Tss] 3 times, Tss 14, Ttop, Te. *25 sts.* RPCC.

Body Section

Row 12: With CC, [Tss, Tmos] 3 times, Tss 17, Te. *25 sts.* RPCC.

Row 13: With MC, [Tmos, Tss] 3 times, Tss 16, Tmos, Te. RPCC.

Row 14: With CC, [Tss, Tmos] 2 times, Tss 17, Tmos, Tss, Te. RPCC.

Row 15: With MC, [Tmos, Tss] 2 times, Tss 16, Tmos, Tss, Tmos, Te. RPCC.

Row 16: With CC, Tss, Tmos, Tss 17, [Tmos, Tss] 2 times, Te. RPCC.

Row 17: With MC, Tmos, Tss 16, [Tss, Tmos] 3 times, Te. RPCC.

Row 18: With CC, Tss 17, [Tmos, Tss] 3 times, Te. RPCC.

Row 19: With MC, Tss 15, [Tss, Tmos] 4 times, Te. RPCC.

Row 20: With CC, Tss 17, [Tmos, Tss] 3 times, Te. RPCC.

Row 21: With MC, Tmos, Tss 16, [Tss, Tmos] 3 times, Te. RPCC.

Row 22: With CC, Tss, Tmos, Tss 17, [Tmos, Tss] 2 times, Te. RPCC.

Row 23: With MC, [Tmos, Tss] 2 times, Tss 16, Tmos, Tss, Tmos, Te. RPCC.

Row 24: With CC, [Tss, Tmos] 2 times, Tss 17, Tmos, Tss, Te. RPCC.

Row 25: With MC, [Tmos, Tss] 3 times, Tss 16, Tmos, Te. RPCC.

Row 26: With CC, [Tss, Tmos] 3 times, Tss 17, Te. RPCC.

Row 27: With MC, [Tmos, Tss] 4 times, Tss 15, Te. RPCC.

Rep Rows 12–27 11 more times for a total of 12 repeats. Adjust length by adding or subtracting reps.

On the last rep of Row 27, work an RPD-CC.

Decrease Section

Row 28: With CC, [Tmos, Tss] 3 times, Tss 15, Te. *23 sts.* RPD-CC.

Row 29: With MC, [Tmos, Tss] 2 times, Tss 13, Tmos, Tss, Te. *21 sts.* RPD-CC.

Row 30: With CC, [Tmos, Tss] 2 times, Tss 13, Te. *19 sts.* RPD-CC.

Row 31: With MC, [Tmos, Tss] 2 times, Tss 11, Te. *17 sts.* RPD-CC.

Row 32: With CC, Tmos, Tss 12, Te. *15 sts.* RPD-CC.

Row 33: With MC, Tss 9, Tmos, Tss, Te. *13 sts.* RPD-CC.

Row 34: With CC, Tss 9, Te. *11 sts.* RPD-CC.

Row 35: With MC, Tmos, Tss 6, Te. *9 sts.* RPD-CC.

Row 36: With CC, Tss 5, Te. *7 sts.* RPD-CC.

Row 37: With MC, Tss 2, Tmos, Te. *5 sts.*

Row 37 RP: Do not ch 1, [yo and pull through 2 loops] rep until 3 loops rem on hook, yo and pull through 3 loops.

Row 38: With MC, Tss, Te. *3 sts.* Yo and pull through all loops.

Finishing

Fasten off and weave in ends. Block gently to remove curl.

Vista Shawl

With purple and blue hues, the Vista Shawl was inspired by the sweeping views of the Blue Mesa Trail in Petrified Forest National Park in northeastern Arizona. The kite shaping accentuates the layers of textures and colors in this versatile shawl. Choose three colors to re-create your favorite scenic overlook. While not required, carrying yarn and using the technique to trap yarn on the return pass will save you from weaving in a lot of yarn ends when finished.

YARN

Birch Hollow Fibers Phillis DK (DK weight); 100% Superwash Merino; 250 yd (229 m) per 4.1 oz (115 g)

Colors:
C1: Grurple; 1 skein, 250 yd (229 m)
C2: Ballgown; 1 skein, 250 yd (229 m)
C3: Amethyst Ocean; 1 skein, 250 yd (229 m)

HOOK

6.5 mm (US K-10.5) Tunisian crochet hook with cable at least 12 in (30 cm) long

NOTIONS

Tapestry needle, removable stitch marker

GAUGE

16 Tss and 16 rows per 4 in (10 cm)

FINISHED SIZE

A: 20 in (50 cm)
B: 70 in (180 cm)

STITCHES AND TECHNIQUES

Tss, Tss2Tog, Tfs, Tmss, Te

Return pass with decrease (RPD): Ch 1, [yo and pull through 2 loops] rep until 1 st before marked st, yo and pull through 4 loops, [yo and pull through 2 loops] rep until 1 loop rem on hook. *2 sts decreased.*

Return pass with decrease and color change (RPD-CC): Ch 1, [yo and pull through 2 loops] rep until 1 st before marked st, yo and pull through 4 loops, [yo and pull through 2 loops] rep until 2 loops rem on hook, drop current color, pick up next color, and then yo and pull through all loops. *2 sts decreased.*

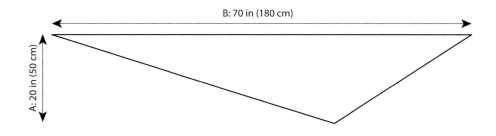

INSTRUCTIONS

Section 1

Notes: *Odd-numbered rows have a 2-stitch increase at the beginning and the end of the FP. Even-numbered rows have a 1-stitch increase at the beginning and end of the FP. All rows have a 2-stitch decrease in the center of the return pass starting in Row 3. Stitch marker is placed in Row 4. Move the stitch marker up each row so it stays in the center decrease. In Section 1, there should always be the same number of loops before and after the marked stitch on the hook before the return pass.*

Foundation Row: With C1, ch 3. Starting in the 2nd ch from hook, pick up a loop in the back bump of all chains. *3 sts.*

Foundation Row RP: Ch 1, [yo and pull through 2 loops] twice.

Row 1: (Tss, Tmss, Tss), Te. *5 sts.*

Note: *The ( ) indicates multiple stitches to be worked in 1 space. On Row 1, work a Tss, then a Tmss, and then a second Tss into the first st.*

Row 1 RP: Ch 1, [yo and pull through 2 loops] rep until 1 loop rem on hook.

Row 2: (Tss, Tmss), Tss, (Tss, Tmss), Te. *7 sts.*

Row 2 RP: Ch 1, [yo and pull through 2 loops] rep until 1 loop rem on hook.

Row 3: (Tss, Tmss), Tss 3, (Tss, Tmss), Te. *9 sts.*

Row 3 RP: Ch 1, [yo and pull through 2 loops] rep until 1 loop rem on hook.

Row 4: (Tss, Tmss), Tss 2, Tss and place marker, Tss 2, (Tss, Tmss), Te. *11 sts.* RPD.

Note: *The marked Tss goes through the 3 sts that were decreased together on the previous return pass. The stitch marker is being used to mark the center of the forward pass and the center of the return pass decrease. Move it up each row.*

Row 5: (Tss, Tmss) 2, Tss 3, (Tss, Tmss) 2, Te. *11 sts.* RPD.

Row 6: (Tss, Tmss), Tss until 2 sts rem, (Tss, Tmss), Te. *+0 sts.* RPD.

Row 7: (Tss, Tmss) 2, Tss until 3 sts rem, (Tss, Tmss) 2, Te. *+2 sts.* RPD.

Rows 8–11: Rep Rows 6–7. *17 sts.*

Row 12: With C2, rep Row 6. *17 sts.* RPD-CC.

Row 13: With C1, rep Row 7. *19 sts.* RPD-CC.

Rows 14–15: With C2, rep Rows 6–7. *21 sts.* RPD-CC.

Rows 16–17: With C1, rep Row 6–7. *23 sts.* RPD-CC.

Rows 18–21: With C2, rep Rows 6–7. *27 sts.* RPD-CC.

Rows 22–25: With C1, rep Rows 6–7. *31 sts.* RPD-CC.

Rows 26–33: With C2, rep Rows 6–7. *39 sts.* RPD-CC.

Row 34: With C3, rep Row 6. *39 sts.* RPD.

Row 35: (Tss, Tmss), Tfs, [Tss2Tog, Tfs] until marked st, Tss, Tfs, [Tss2Tog, Tfs] rep until 2 sts rem, (Tss, Tmss), Te. *+2 sts.* RPD.

Note: *Tfs is worked in the space before the next set of vertical bars and is used as an increase in this pattern.*

Row 36: (Tss, Tmss), [Tfs, Tss2Tog] until 1 st before marked st, Tss 3, [Tss2Tog, Tfs] rep until 2 sts rem, (Tss, Tmss), Te. *+0 sts.* RPD.

Row 37: (Tss, Tmss) 2, [Tfs, Tss2Tog] until marked st, Tss, [Tss2Tog, Tfs] rep until 3 sts rem, (Tss, Tmss) 2, Te. *+2 sts.* RPD.

Row 38: (Tss, Tmss), [Tfs, Tss2Tog] until marked st, Tss, [Tss2Tog, Tfs] rep until 2 sts rem, (Tss, Tmss), Te. *+0 sts.* RPD.

Rows 39–46: Rep Rows 35–38 twice. *51 sts.*

Row 47: Rep Row 35. *53 sts.* RPD-CC.

Row 48: With C1, rep Row 36. *53 sts.*

Row 49: With C1, rep Row 7. *55 sts.*

Rows 50–55: With C1, rep Rows 6–7. *61 sts.*

Rows 56–92: Rep Rows 12–48. *97 sts.*

Section 2

Rows 93–99: With C1, Tss until 2 sts rem, (Tss, Tmss), Te. *–1 st/row.* RPD-CC.

Row 100: With C2, Tss until 2 sts rem, (Tss, Tmss), Te. *89 sts.* RPD-CC.

Row 101: With C1, Tss until 2 sts rem, (Tss, Tmss), Te. *88 sts.* RPD-CC.

Rows 102–103: With C2, Tss until 2 sts rem, (Tss, Tmss), Te. *86 sts.* RPD-CC.

Rows 104–105: With C1, Tss until 2 sts rem, (Tss, Tmss), Te. *84 sts.* RPD-CC.

Rows 106–109: With C2, Tss until 2 sts rem, (Tss, Tmss), Te. *80 sts.* RPD-CC.

Rows 110–113: With C1, Tss until 2 sts rem, (Tss, Tmss), Te. *76 sts.* RPD-CC.

Rows 114–121: With C2, Tss until 2 sts rem, (Tss, Tmss), Te. *68 sts.* RPD-CC.

Row 122: With C3, Tss until 2 sts rem, (Tss, Tmss), Te. *67 sts*. RPD.

Row 123: [Tss2Tog, Tfs] rep to marked st, Tss 2, [Tfs, Tss2Tog] rep until 2 sts rem, (Tss, Tmss), Te. *66 sts*. RPD.

Row 124: [Tss2Tog, Tfs] rep to 1 st before marked st, Tss 3, [Tfs, Tss2Tog] rep until 2 sts rem, (Tss, Tmss), Te. *65 sts*. RPD.

Rows 125–136: Rep Rows 123–124 6 times. *53 sts*.

Row 137: Rep Row 123. *52 sts*.

Row 138: Tss 3, [Tfs, Tss2Tog] rep until 2 sts rem, (Tss, Tmss), Te. *51 sts*. RPD.

Bind off: SlstBO as follows: Tss, [Tfs, Tss2Tog] rep until 2 sts rem, Tss, Te.

Finishing

Fasten off and weave in ends. Block gently to remove curl and open up the lace bands.

Compass Shawl

If you're looking for a shawl that is both elegant and warm, the Compass Shawl is the perfect choice. This shallow, center-out triangle shawl swaps between the main color (MC) and the contrast color (CC) at the end of the forward pass to create the stunning colorwork bands. The shallow triangle shape is created by increasing at the beginning and end of the forward pass on every row while only increasing at the center on the even rows.

YARN
Kim Dyes Yarn Tartlet Sport (Sport weight); 100% Superwash Merino; 385 yd (352 m) per 3.6 oz (103 g)

Colors:
MC: Oxblood; 2 skeins, 700 yd (640 m)
CC: Silver Lining; 1 skein, 200 yd (183 m)

HOOK
5.5 mm (US I-9) Tunisian crochet hook with cable at least 16 in (40 cm) long.

NOTIONS
Tapestry needle, removable stitch marker

GAUGE
20 Tss and 20 rows per 4 in (10 cm)

FINISHED SIZE
A: 20 in (50 cm)
B: 60 in (150 cm)

STITCHES AND TECHNIQUES
MR, Tss, Tks, Tmss, Twup, Te

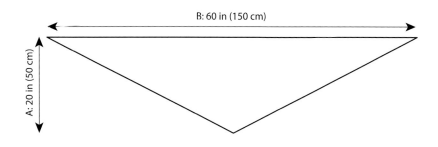

INSTRUCTIONS

Foundation Row: With MC, [insert hook into MR, pull up a loop, ch 1] 5 times. *5 sts.*

Foundation Row RP and all following RP: Work a standard RP.

Row 1: (Tss, Tmss), (Tks, Tss, Tks), (Tss, Tmss), Te. *9 sts.*

Row 2: (Tss, Tmss), Tss 2, Tks, Tss 2, (Tss, Tmss), Te. *11 sts.*

Row 3: (Tss, Tmss), Tss 3, (Tks, Tss, Tks), Tss 3, (Tss, Tmss), Te. *15 sts.*

Row 4: (Tss, Tmss), Tss 5, Tks and pm, Tss 5, (Tss, Tmss), Te. *17 sts.*

Note: *The stitch marker is used to mark the center of the row. There will always be an equal number of stitches before and after it. Carry the stitch marker up each row. For even rows, it moves to the Tks. For odd rows, it moves to the Tss in the center of the (Tks, Tss, Tks).*

Row 5: (Tss, Tmss), Tss to marked st, (Tks, Tss, Tks) in marked st, Tss until 2 sts rem, (Tss, Tmss), Te. *21 sts.*

Row 6: (Tss, Tmss), Tss to marked st, Tks in marked st, Tss until 2 sts rem, (Tss, Tmss), Te. *23 sts.*

Row 7: Rep Row 5.

Row 8: (Tss, Tmss), Tss to marked st, Tks in marked st, Tss until 2 sts rem, (Tss, Tmss), with CC, Te. *29 sts.*

Note: *When a row has a color change, it is always at the Te. Drop the current color, pick up the next color, and then Te and continue with the RP.*

Row 9: (Tss, Tmss), [Twup, Tss] rep to marked st, (Tks, Tss, Tks) in marked st, [Twup, Tss] rep until 2 sts rem, (Tss, Tmss), with MC, Te. *33 sts.*

Note: *For Rows 10–14, the stitches line up with the prior row. Tss is worked into Tss. Twup is worked into Twup.*

Row 10: (Tss, Tmss), [Tss, Twup] rep to marked st, Tks in marked st, [Tss, Twup] rep until 2 sts rem, (Tss, Tmss), with CC, Te. *35 sts.*

Row 11: (Tss, Tmss), Twup, [Tss, Twup] rep to marked st, (Tks, Tss, Tks) in marked st, Tss, [Twup, Tss] rep until 2 sts rem, (Tss, Tmss), with MC, Te. *39 sts.*

Row 12: (Tss, Tmss), Tss, [Twup, Tss] rep to marked st, Tks in marked st, Twup, [Tss, Twup] rep until 2 sts rem, (Tss, Tmss), with CC, Te. *41 sts.*

Row 13: Rep Row 9.

Row 14: Rep Row 10 but do not change color. Use MC for Te and RP.

Two-color band in Rows 9–14

Rows 15–18: Rep Rows 5–6.

Row 19: Rep Row 5.

Row 20: Rep Row 8.

Row 21: (Tss, Tmss), [Twup, Tss] rep to marked st, (Tks, Tss, Tks) in marked st, [Twup, Tss] rep until 2 sts rem, (Tss, Tmss), with MC, Te.

Note: For Rows 22–26, the stitches alternate with the prior row. Tss is worked into Twup. Twup is worked into Tss.

Row 22: (Tss, Tmss), [Twup, Tss] rep to marked st, Tks in marked st, [Twup, Tss] rep until 2 sts rem, (Tss, Tmss), with CC, Te.

Row 23: (Tss, Tmss), Twup, [Tss, Twup] rep to marked st, (Tks, Tss, Tks) in marked st, Tss, [Twup, Tss] rep until 2 sts rem, (Tss, Tmss), with MC, Te.

Row 24: (Tss, Tmss), Twup, [Tss, Twup] rep to marked st, Tks in marked st, Tss, [Twup, Tss] rep until 2 sts rem, (Tss, Tmss), with CC, Te.

Row 25: Rep Row 21.

Row 26: Rep Row 22 but do not change color. Use MC for Te and RP.

Two-color band in Rows 21–26

Rows 27–32: Rep Rows 15–20.

Rows 33–80: Rep Rows 9–32 twice. For a larger shawl, work additional repeats.

Rows 81–85: Rep Rows 9–13. Fasten off CC.

Bind off: Using a scBO, work the row as Tss, [Tss, Twup] rep to marked st, Tks in marked st, [Tss, Twup] rep until 2 sts rem, Tss, Te. Fasten off MC.

Finishing

Weave in all ends, block gently.

Wandering Path Scarf

Full of warmth and texture, this cabled scarf—in your choice of two lengths—is sure to keep you cozy while roaming through the woods. This scarf is a great introduction to Tunisian crochet cables because all the cables are worked over either 3 or 4 stitches, making it easier to keep track of all the stitches.

YARN
Camellia Fiber Company CFC Merino Worsted (Worsted weight); 100% superfine merino wool; 215 yd (196.6 m) per 3.5 oz (100 g)

Color: Chicory; 2 skeins, 430 yd (393.2 m), or 3 skeins, 625 yd (571.5 m)

HOOK
6.5 mm (US K-10.5) Tunisian crochet hook at least 6 in (15 cm) long

6.5 mm (US K-10.5) crochet hook for cables

NOTIONS
Tapestry needle, removable stitch marker

GAUGE
14 Tss and 14 rows per 4 in (10 cm)
Note: Cable stitches will change the st gauge and shrinkage is expected.

FINISHED SIZE
A: 7 in (18 cm)
B: 52 in (130 cm) or 78 in (200 cm)

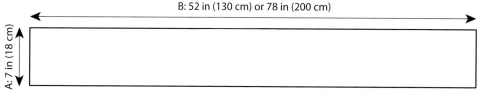

B: 52 in (130 cm) or 78 in (200 cm)

A: 7 in (18 cm)

STITCHES AND TECHNIQUES
Tss, Tks, Tps, Ptrs, Te

CABLE STITCHES

2/1F—2 over 1 front cable (worked over next 3 sts): With the second hook, Tks in the next 2 sts and hold hook in front of fabric. With main hook, Tss in the next st, and then transfer the stitches on the second hook to the main hook. Alternative method: Skip the next 2 sets of vertical bars. Tss in third set of vertical bars (photo 1). Tks in first set of vertical bars (photo 2), Tks in second set of vertical bars (photo 3).

Tss in third set of vertical bars

Tks in first set of vertical bars

Tks in second set of vertical bars

2/1B—2 over 1 back cable (worked over next 3 sts): With second hook, Tss in first st and move to back of fabric. With the main hook, Tks in next 2 sts (photo 4). Move loop from second hook to main hook.

2/1B

2/2B—2 over 2 back cable (worked over next 4 sts): With second hook, Tks in the next 2 sts and move to back of fabric. With main hook, Tks in next 2 sts (photo 5). Move loops from second hook to main hook.

2/2B

Note: *Because of the nature of cables (crossing over etc.), there will be times where you have to search/dig around for the next set of vertical bars. Looking at the chains of the return pass can be helpful in finding stitches and/or determining the correct order to work the stitches.*

ADJUSTING LENGTH

The length of the scarf is easily adjustable. Record the weight of the scarf after completing Row 18. This is the amount of yarn needed to complete 1 repeat and the last 5 rows. After completing a repeat (Rows 7–18), weigh the remaining yarn.

If you have more than the amount recorded, there is enough yarn to complete another repeat; otherwise, continue on to Row 19 to work the last 5 rows of the scarf.

INSTRUCTIONS

Foundation Row: Ch 32. Starting in the 2nd ch from hook, pick up a loop in the back bump of all chains. *32 sts.*

Foundation Row RP and all following RP: Work a standard RP.

Row 1: Ptrs 30, Te. *32 sts.*

Row 2: Tps 30, Te.

Row 3: Tss 8, Tks 2, Tps 10, Tks 2, Tss 8, Te.

Row 4: Tps 8, Tks 2, Tps 10, Tks 2, Tps 8, Te.

Rows 5–6: Tss 4, Tks 2, Tps 2, Tks 2, Tps 10, Tks 2, Tps 2, Tks 2, Tss 4, Te.

Row 7: Tss 4, 2/1F, Tps, 2/1F, Tps 8, 2/1B, Tps, 2/1B, Tss 4, Te.

Row 8: Tss 5, 2/1F, Tps, 2/1F, Tps 6, 2/1B, Tps, 2/1B, Tss 5, Te.

Row 9: Tss 6, 2/1F, Tps, 2/1F, Tps 4, 2/1B, Tps, 2/1B, Tss 6, Te.

Row 10: Tss 7, 2/1F, Tps, 2/1F, Tps 2, 2/1B, Tps, 2/1B, Tss 7, Te.

Row 11: Tss 8, 2/1F, Tps, 2/1F, 2/1B, Tps, 2/1B, Tss 8, Te.

Row 12: Tss 9, Tks 2, Tps 2, 2/2B, Tps 2, Tks 2, Tss 9, Te.

Hint: *The Tks stitches for the first 2/1F in Row 13 tend to hide in the back and it may be easier to use the second hook method for this stitch.*

Row 13: Tss 8, 2/1B, Tps, 2/1B, 2/1F, Tps, 2/1F, Tss 8, Te.

Row 14: Tss 7, 2/1B, Tps, 2/1B, Tps 2, 2/1F, Tps, 2/1F, Tss 7, Te.

Row 15: Tss 6, 2/1B, Tps, 2/1B, Tps 4, 2/1F, Tps, 2/1F, Tss 6, Te.

Row 16: Tss 5, 2/1B, Tps, 2/1B, Tps 6, 2/1F, Tps, 2/1F, Tss 5, Te.

Row 17: Tss 4, 2/1B, Tps, 2/1B, Tps 8, 2/1F, Tps, 2/1F, Tss 4, Te.

Row 18: Tss 4, Tks 2, Tps 2, Tks 2, Tps 10, Tks 2, Tps 2, Tks 2, Tss 4, Te.

Rep Rows 7–18 a further 11 (18) times for a 2 (3) skein scarf or until you have enough yarn left to work 5 more rows.

Row 19: Tss 4, Tks 2, Tps 2, Tks 2, Tps 10, Tks 2, Tps 2, Tks 2, Tss 4, Te.

Row 20: Tps 8, Tks 2, Tps 10, Tks 2, Tps 8, Te.

Row 21: Tss 8, Tks 2, Tps 10, Tks 2, Tss 8, Te.

Row 22: Tps 30, Te.

Row 23: SlstBO with Ptrs 30, slstBO with Te.

Finishing

Fasten off and weave in ends. Block gently to remove curl.

Stargazer Shawl

This dramatic lace shawl is the perfect accessory for a night out in warm weather. The Stargazer Shawl is worked from the bottom up using a three-row repeat to create this stunning lace pattern. The lace pattern requires a return pass with both increases and decreases. Practicing with the gauge swatch is highly recommended.

YARN
Lolabean Yarn Co. Pinto Bean (DK weight); 100% Superwash Merino; 250 yd (229 m) per 4.1 oz (115 g)

Color: Purple Nurple; 3 skeins, 750 yd (686 m)

HOOK
6.5 mm (US K-10.5) Tunisian crochet hook with 16 in (40 cm) or longer cable

NOTIONS
Tapestry needle

GAUGE
2 rep of [Tss 3, (Ttop, yo, Ttop)] and 8 rows per 4 in (10 cm)

PATTERN FOR GAUGE
It can be tempting to skip the gauge swatch for a shawl pattern. This gauge swatch, however, is useful for a few reasons: 1) This lace pattern expands a lot when blocking. Making a gauge swatch is useful for determining whether the hook size used will create the desired look. 2) Measure before and after blocking so you know how much it will expand. This shawl is highly adjustable, so this lets you know when it will be the right size for you. 3) This is a great way to practice with the lace stitch pattern before jumping into the shawl.

Swatch before blocking

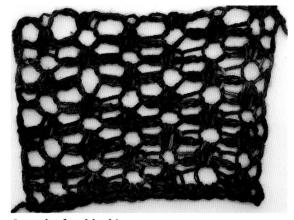

Swatch after blocking

Foundation Row: Ch 20. Starting in the 2nd ch from hook, pick up a loop in the back bump of all chains. *20 sts.*

Foundation Row RP: Ch 1, *ch 1, yo and pull through 4 loops, ch 1, [yo and pull through 2 loops] 3 times; rep from * until 2 loops rem, [yo and pull through 2 loops].

Row 1: [Tss 3, (Ttop, yo, Ttop)] 3 times, Te.

Row 1 RP: Ch 1, *[yo and pull through 2 loops] 3 times, ch 1, yo and pull through 4 loops, ch 1; rep from * until 2 loops rem, [yo and pull through 2 loops].

(Ttop, yo, Ttop) location

Row 2: [(Ttop, yo, Ttop), Tss 3] 3 times, Te.

Row 2 RP: Ch 1, *ch1, yo and pull through 4 loops, ch 1, [yo and pull through 2 loops] 3 times; rep from * until 2 loops rem, [yo and pull through 2 loops].

Rep Rows 1–2.

FINISHED SIZE

A: 75 in (190 cm)
B: 50 in (130 cm)

STITCHES AND TECHNIQUES

MR, Tss, Tks, Ttop, Te

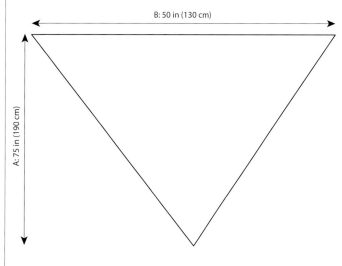

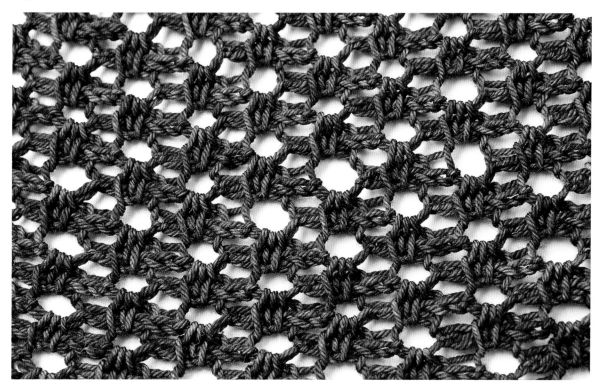

INSTRUCTIONS

Foundation Row: [Insert hook into MR, yo and pull up a loop, ch 1] 3 times. *3 sts.*

Foundation Row RP and all following RP unless stated otherwise: Work a standard RP.

Row 1: Ttop, Tss, Ttop, Te. *5 sts.*

Row 2: Tss, yo, Tss, yo, Tss, Te. *7 sts.*

Row 3: Tss, yo, Tks, Tss, Tks, yo, Tss, Te. *9 sts.*

Row 3 RP: Ch 1, [yo and pull through 2 loops] twice, ch 1, yo and pull through 4 loops, ch 1, [yo and pull through 2 loops] 3 times.

Row 4: Tss, yo, Tks, (Ttop, yo, Ttop), Tks, yo, Tss, Te. *11 sts.*

Row 5: Tss, yo, Tks, Tss 5, Tks, yo, Tss, Te. *13 sts.*

Row 5 RP: Ch 1, [yo and pull through 2 loops] 4 times, ch 1, yo and pull through 4 loops, ch 1, [yo and pull through 2 loops] 5 times.

Row 6: Tss, yo, Tks, Tss 2, (Ttop, yo, Ttop), Tss 2, Tks, yo, Tss, Te. *15 sts.*

Row 6 RP: Ch 1, [yo and pull through 2 loops] 2 times, *ch 1, yo and pull through 4 loops, ch 1, [yo and pull through 2 loops] 3 times; rep from * once more.

Row 7: Tss, yo, Tks, (Ttop, yo, Ttop), [Tss 3, (Ttop, yo, Ttop)] rep until 3 sts rem, Tks, yo, Tss, Te. *+2 sts.*

Row 7 RP: Ch 1, [yo and pull through 2 loops] 6 times, *ch 1, yo and pull through 4 loops, ch 1, [yo and pull through 2 loops] 3 times; rep from * until 5 loops rem on hook, [yo and pull through 2 loops] 4 times.

Row 8: Tss, yo, Tks, Tss 4, [(Ttop, yo, Ttop), Tss 3] rep until 4 sts rem, Tss, Tks, yo, Tss, Te. *+2 sts.*

Row 8 RP: Ch 1, [yo and pull through 2 loops] 4 times, *ch 1, yo and pull through 4 loops, ch 1, [yo and pull through 2 loops] 3 times; rep from * until 3 loops rem on hook, [yo and pull through 2 loops] twice.

Row 9: Tss, yo, Tks, Tss 2, (Ttop, yo, Ttop), [Tss 3, (Ttop, yo, Ttop)] rep until 5 sts rem, Tss 2, Tks, yo, Tss, Te. *+2 sts.*

Row 9 RP: Ch 1, [yo and pull through 2 loops] twice, *ch 1, yo and pull through 4 loops, ch 1, [yo and pull through 2 loops] 3 times; rep from *.

Rows 10–99: Rep Rows 7–9 30 more times. For a larger shawl, work more repeats before continuing to bind off. Each repeat adds another 6 sts.

Row 99 RP: Work a standard return pass.

Bind off: Work a stretchy bind-off with Tss.

FINISHING

Fasten off and weave in ends. Block enthusiastically to open up the lace stitches.

Trailblazer
Shawl

The Trailblazer Shawl is perfect for the ambitious Tunisian crocheter who loves texture and is eager to try new stitch patterns. Each band of this cozy, center-out triangle explores a new stitch pattern that will keep you intrigued.

YARN
Cascade 220 Merino (Worsted weight); 100% merino; 220 yd (201 m) per 3.5 oz (100 g)

Color: 50 Blue Shadow; 3 skeins, 660 yd (603.5 m)

HOOK
6.5 mm (US K-10.5) hook with cable at least 16 in (40 cm) long

NOTIONS
Tapestry needle, removable stitch marker

GAUGE
14 Tss and 15 rows per 4 in (10 cm)

FINISHED SIZE
A: 24 in (60 cm)
B: 60 in (150 cm)

STITCHES AND TECHNIQUES
MR, Tss, Tbss, Tks, Tmfs, Trs, Tps, Twd, Twup, Te

Tunisian cross stitch (Tx): This is a stitch worked over the next 2 stitches. Skip the first stitch and Tss into the second stitch (photo 1), and then Tss in the first stitch (photo 2).

Tss into the second stitch

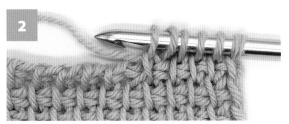

Tss in the first stitch

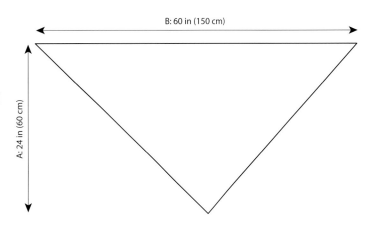

INSTRUCTIONS

Foundation Row: [Insert hook into MR, pull up a loop, ch 1] 5 times. *5 sts.*

Foundation Row RP and all following RP: Work a standard RP.

Row 1: Tmfs, Tss, (Tss, Tks, Tss) in next st, Tss, Tmfs, Te. *9 sts.*

Row 2: Tmfs, Tss 3, (Tss, Tks, Tss) in next st, Tss 3, Tmfs, Te. *13 sts.*

Row 3: Tmfs, Tss 5, (Tss, Tks, Tss) in next st, Tss 5, Tmfs, Te. *17 sts.*

Row 4: Tmfs, Tss 7, (Tss, Tks, Tss) in next st, Tss 7, Tmfs, Te. *21 sts.*

Row 5: Tmfs, Tss 9, (Tss, Tks, Tss) in next st, Tss 9, Tmfs, Te. *25 sts.*

Row 6: Tmfs, Tss 11, (Tss, Tks, Tss) in next st, Tss 11, Tmfs, Te. *29 sts.*

Row 7: Tmfs, Tss 13, (Tss, Tks, Tss) in next st, Tss 13, Tmfs, Te. *33 sts.*

Row 8: Tmfs, Tss 15, (Tss, Tks, Tss) in next st, Tss 15, Tmfs, Te. *37 sts.*

Row 9: Tmfs, Tss 17, (Tss, Tks, Tss) in next st, Tss 17, Tmfs, Te. *41 sts.*

Row 10: Tmfs, Trs 19, (Tss, Tks, Tss) in next st, Trs 19, Tmfs, Te. *45 sts.*

Row 11: Tmfs, Tss, [Tbss, Tss] 10 times, (Tss, Tks and pm, Tss) in next st, Tss, [Tbss, Tss] 10 times, Tmfs, Te. *49 sts.*

Note: For all remaining rows, move the marker up to the center Tks st.

Note: For Rows 12–19, Tss stitches are worked into Tss stitches and the Tbss stitches are worked into Tbss stitches (photo 3).

For Rows 12–19, Tss stitches are worked into Tss stitches and the Tbss stitches are worked into Tbss stitches.

Row 12: Tmfs, Tbss, [Tss, Tbss] until marked st, (Tss, Tks, Tss) in next st, Tbss, [Tss, Tbss] rep until 1 st rem, Tmfs, Te. *53 sts.*

Row 13: Tmfs, Tss, [Tbss, Tss] until marked st, (Tss, Tks, Tss) in next st, Tss, [Tbss, Tss] rep until 1 st rem, Tmfs, Te. *57 sts.*

Rows 14–19: Rep Rows 12–13 3 times.

Row 20: Tmfs, Trs 39, (Tss, Tks, Tss) in next st, Trs 39, Tmfs, Te. *85 sts.*

Row 21: Tmfs, Tss, [Tps, Tss] 20 times, (Tss, Tks, Tss) in next st, Tss, [Tps, Tss] 20 times, Tmfs, Te. *89 sts.*

Note: *For Rows 22–29, Tps stitches are worked into Tss stitches while Tss stitches are worked into Tps stitches. This stitch combo is often referred to as the honeycomb stitch, though there are many alternating stitch combos that could be considered a honeycomb stitch (photo 4).*

Row 22: Tmfs, Tss, [Tps, Tss] rep until marked st, (Tss, Tks, Tss) in next st, Tss, [Tps, Tss] rep until 1 st rem, Tmfs, Te. *93 sts.*

For Rows 22–29, Tps stitches are worked into Tss stitches while Tss stitches are worked into Tps stitches.

Rows 23–29: Rep Row 22.

Row 30: Tmfs, Trs 59, (Tss, Tks, Tss) in next st, Trs 59, Tmfs, Te. *125 sts.*

Row 31: Tmfs, Tx 30, Tss, (Tss, Tks, Tss) in next st, Tss, Tx 30, Tmfs, Te. *129 sts.*

Note: *For Rows 32–39, the Tx stitch is worked into the same set of vertical bars as the previous row (photo 5).*

For Rows 32–39, the Tx stitch is worked into the same set of vertical bars as the previous row.

Row 32: Tmfs, Tss, Tx to marked st, (Tss, Tks, Tss) in next st, Tx until 2 sts rem, Tss, Tmfs, Te. *133 sts.*

Row 33: Tmfs, Tx to 1 st before marked st, Tss, (Tss, Tks, Tss) in next st, Tss, Tx until 1 st rem, Tmfs, Te. *137 sts.*

Rows 34–39: Rep Rows 32–33.

Row 40: Tmfs, Trs 79, (Tss, Tks, Tss) in next st, Trs 79, Tmfs, Te. *165 sts.*

Note: *For Rows 41–49, Twd stitches are worked into Tks stitches while Tks stitches are worked into Twd stitches (photo 6).*

Rows 41–49: Tmfs, Tks, [Twd, Tks] rep until marked st, (Tss, Tks, Tss) in next st, Tks, [Twd, Tks] rep until 1 st rem, Tmfs, Te.

For Rows 41–49, Twd stitches are worked into Tks stitches while Tks stitches are worked into Twd stitches.

Row 50: Tmfs, Trs 99, (Tss, Tks, Tss) in next st, Trs 99, Tmfs, Te. *205 sts.*

Row 51: Tmfs, Tss, [Twup, Tss] rep until marked st, (Tss, Tks, Tss) in next st, Tss, [Twup, Tss] rep until 1 st rem, Tmfs, Te. *209 sts.*

Row 52: Tmfs, Twup, [Tss, Twup] until marked st, (Tss, Tks, Tss) in next st, Twup, [Tss, Twup] rep until 1 st rem, Tmfs, Te. *213 sts.*

Rows 53–58: Rep Rows 51–52 3 times.

Row 59: Rep Row 51. *241 sts.*

Row 60: Work a slstBO in Trs.

Finishing

Fasten off and weave in ends. Block gently to remove curl.

Treeline
Mitts

Fingerless mitts are my favorite fall accessory. They keep my hands warm without hindering the use of my fingers. The Treeline fingerless mitts are worked flat from the bottom up and then sewn after blocking. These mitts are great for practicing getting gauge with a stitch pattern and for learning the lattice stitch pattern [Tss2Tog, yu] before trying these skills in the round with the matching hat.

YARN
Cascade 220 (Worsted weight); 100% Peruvian Highland wool; 220 yd (201 m) per 3.5 oz (100 g)

Color: 1006 Sky Blue; 1 skein, 100 yd (91.4 m)

HOOK
6 mm (US J-10) Tunisian crochet hook at least 6 in (40 cm) long

NOTIONS
Tapestry needle

GAUGE
8 repeats of [Tss, Twup] and 16 rows per 4 in (10 cm)

SIZES
Small, (Medium, Large) to fit palm circumference of 7 (7.5, 8) in/18 (19, 20) cm

FINISHED SIZE
Small (Medium, Large)
A: 6 (6, 6) in/15 (15, 15) cm
B: 6.5 (7, 7.5) in/16 (17.5, 19) cm

STITCHES AND TECHNIQUES
Tss, Tss2Tog, Twup, Te

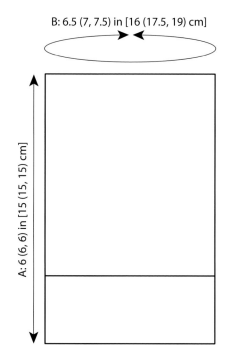

B: 6.5 (7, 7.5) in [16 (17.5, 19) cm]

A: 6 (6, 6) in [15 (15, 15) cm]

INSTRUCTIONS

Foundation Row: Ch 26 (28, 30). Starting in the 2nd ch from hook, pick up a loop in the back bump of all chains. *26 (28, 30) sts.*

Foundation Row RP: For this and all following RP, work a standard RP.

Rows 1–4: [Tss, Twup] rep until last st, Te.

Note: *A yarn under (yu) is similar to a yarn over (yo), but you wrap the yarn in the opposite direction (photo 1).*

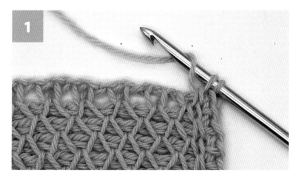

Yarn under

Hint: *In Row 5, you will want to use the index finger on your hook hand to hold the yu to keep it from falling off the hook while working the stitch that follows it (photo 2).*

Use the index finger on your hook hand to hold the yu while working the stitch that follows it.

Row 5: [Tss2Tog, yu] rep until last st, Te.

Note: *The Tss2Tog in Row 6 goes through the front loop from a yu and then the Tss2Tog (photos 3 and 4).*

The Tss2Tog goes through the front loop of the yu and the next vertical bar.

Completed Tss2Tog

Row 6: Tss, [Tss2Tog, yu] rep until 2 sts rem, Tss, Te.
Rows 7–20: Rep Rows 5–6.
Adjusting length: For longer or shorter mitts, adjust the number of repeats of Rows 5–6.
Row 21: [Tss2Tog, yu] rep until last st, Te.
Rows 22–23: [Tss, Twup] rep until last st, Te.
Row 24: SlstBO [Tss, Twup] rep until last st, slstBO Te.

FINISHING

Leaving a long tail for sewing, fasten off. Block to finished size.

Sew: Starting at the top of the mitten (Row 24), sew together the edge stitches for the first 5 rows, skip the next 8 rows for the thumb opening (weave the yarn tail through on the back side), and then continue sewing all remaining edge stitches together. Fasten off and weave in ends.

Make second mitt following the same instructions.

Treeline Hat

Ready to adventure into Tunisian crochet in the round? The Treeline Hat is worked from the brim to crown using a double-ended hook and two strands of yarn. One strand of yarn is used for the forward pass and one strand is used for the return pass. Cake your yarn into two balls or use both ends of a center-pull cake. The Treeline Hat uses the lattice stitch pattern explained in the matching Treeline Mitts pattern (pages 121–24).

YARN
Cascade 220 (Worsted weight); 100% Peruvian Highland wool; 220 yd (201 m) per 3.5 oz (100 g)

Color: 1006 Sky Blue; 1 skein, 220 yd (201 m)

HOOK
6 mm (US J-10) Tunisian crochet hook with cable at least 8 in (20 cm) long

6 mm (US J-10) double-ended hook

NOTIONS
Tapestry needle, removable stitch marker

GAUGE
8 reps of [Tss, Twup] and 16 rows per 4 in (10 cm)

SIZES
Small (Medium, Large) for head circumference of 20 (22, 24) in/50 (55, 60) cm

FINISHED SIZE
Small (Medium, Large)
A: 6 (6, 6) in/15 (15, 15) cm
B: 19 (21, 23) in/48 (53, 58) cm

STITCHES AND TECHNIQUES
Tss, Tss2Tog, Twup, Tunisian crochet in the round

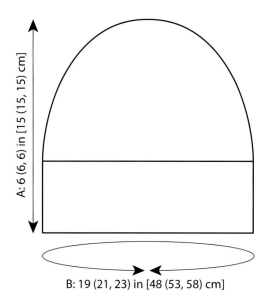

A: 6 (6, 6) in [15 (15, 15) cm]

B: 19 (21, 23) in [48 (53, 58) cm]

INSTRUCTIONS

Foundation Row: Using hook with cable, ch 76 (84, 92). Starting in the 2nd ch from hook, pick up a loop in the back bump of all chains. *76 (84, 92) sts.*

Foundation Row RP: Work a standard return pass, and then place stitch marker in loop on hook. Switch to double-ended hook. Move stitch marker up each rnd.

Brim

Rnd 1: [Twup, Tss] rep.

Rnd 1 RP and all following RP: Work a standard in the round return pass.

Rnd 2: Being careful not to twist, join with Tss to first stitch (marked stitch), move marker to stitch just made. Twup, [Tss, Twup] rep.

Rnds 3–4: [Tss, Twup] rep.

Hat Body

Rnd 5: Tss3Tog, yu, [Tss2Tog, yu] rep until 1 st rem, Tss2Tog in last st and first st of next rnd. *75, (83, 91) sts.*

Rnd 6: Yu, [Tss2Tog, yu] rep.

Rnd 7: [Tss2Tog, yu] rep. until 1 st rem. Tss2Tog in last st and first st of next rnd.

Rnds 8–24: Rep Rnds 6–7.

Crown

SMALL SIZE ONLY

Rnd 1: Tss2Tog, [Tss2Tog, yu] 7 times, Tss2Tog 2, [Tss2Tog, yu] 8 times, Tss2Tog 2, [Tss2Tog, yu] 7 times, Tss2Tog 2, [Tss2Tog, yu] 8 times, Tss. *68 sts.*

Go to All Sizes Rnd 1.

MEDIUM SIZE ONLY

Rnd 1: Tss2Tog, [Tss2Tog, yu] 8 times, Tss2Tog 2, [Tss2Tog, yu] 9 times, Tss2Tog 2, [Tss2Tog, yu] 8 times, Tss2Tog 2, [Tss2Tog, yu] 9 times, Tss. *76 sts.*

Rnd 2: Tss2Tog, [Tss2Tog, yu] 7 times, Tss2Tog 2, [Tss2Tog, yu] 8 times, Tss2Tog 2, [Tss2Tog, yu] 7 times, Tss2Tog 2, [Tss2Tog, yu] 8 times, Tss2Tog. *68 sts.*

Go to All Sizes Rnd 1.

LARGE SIZE ONLY

Rnd 1: Tss2Tog, [Tss2Tog, yu] 9 times, Tss2Tog 2, [Tss2Tog, yu] 10 times, Tss2Tog 2, [Tss2Tog, yu] 9 times, Tss2Tog 2, [Tss2Tog, yu] 10 times, Tss. *84 sts.*

Rnd 2: Tss2Tog, [Tss2Tog, yu] 8 times, Tss2Tog 2, [Tss2Tog, yu] 9 times, Tss2Tog 2, [Tss2Tog, yu] 8 times, Tss2Tog 2, [Tss2Tog, yu] 9 times, Tss2Tog. *76 sts.*

Rnd 3: Tss2Tog, [Tss2Tog, yu] 7 times, Tss2Tog 2, [Tss2Tog, yu] 8 times, Tss2Tog 2, [Tss2Tog, yu] 7 times, Tss2Tog 2, [Tss2Tog, yu] 8 times, Tss2Tog. *68 sts.*

Go to All Sizes Rnd 1.

ALL SIZES

Rnd 1: Tss2Tog, [Tss2Tog, yu] 6 times, Tss2Tog 2, [Tss2Tog, yu] 7 times, Tss2Tog 2, [Tss2Tog, yu] 6 times, Tss2Tog 2, [Tss2Tog, yu] 7 times, Tss2Tog. *60 sts.*

Rnd 2: Tss2Tog, [Tss2Tog, yu] 5 times, Tss2Tog 2, [Tss2Tog, yu] 6 times, Tss2Tog 2, [Tss2Tog, yu] 5 times, Tss2Tog 2, [Tss2Tog, yu] 6 times, Tss2Tog. *52 sts.*

Rnd 3: Tss2Tog, [Tss2Tog, yu] 4 times, Tss2Tog 2, [Tss2Tog, yu] 5 times, Tss2Tog 2, [Tss2Tog, yu] 4 times, Tss2Tog 2, [Tss2Tog, yu] 5 times, Tss2Tog. *44 sts.*

Rnd 4: Tss2Tog, [Tss2Tog, yu] 3 times, Tss2Tog 2, [Tss2Tog, yu] 4 times, Tss2Tog 2, [Tss2Tog, yu] 3 times, Tss2Tog 2, [Tss2Tog, yu] 4 times, Tss2Tog. *36 sts.*

Rnd 5: Tss2Tog, [Tss2Tog, yu] twice, Tss2Tog 2, [Tss2Tog, yu] 3 times, Tss2Tog 2, [Tss2Tog, yu] twice, Tss2Tog 2, [Tss2Tog, yu] 3 times, Tss2Tog. *28 sts.*

Rnd 6: Tss2Tog 2, yu, Tss2Tog 2, [Tss2Tog, yu] twice, Tss2Tog 2, Tss2Tog, yu, Tss2Tog 2, [Tss2Tog, yu] twice, Tss2Tog. *20 sts.*

Rnd 7: Tss2Tog 3, Tss2Tog, yu, Tss2Tog 4, Tss2Tog, yu, Tss2Tog. *12 sts.*

Rnd 8: Tss2Tog 6. *6 sts.*

Finishing

Cut both yarns, leaving at least a 6 in (15 cm) tail. Thread both yarns into a tapestry needle. Insert needle as if to Tss through all 6 stitches and pull to tighten. Thread yarn through top to inside. Fasten off. Use tail on hat brim to sew the Foundation Row gap closed. Weave in all ends. Block gently to reduce any curl at brim.

Crossroads Cowl

Make a statement with this stunning two-color cowl. Tunisian crochet in the round really shines when different colors are used for the forward and return passes. The Crossroads Cowl creates a fabric similar to brioche knitting. Pick your two favorite colors to create an accessory that you'll keep reaching for over and over.

YARN
KnittinBro DK (DK weight); 100% Superwash Merino; 231 yd (211.2 m) per 3.5 oz (100 g)

Sample 1 Colors
MC: Split Cedar; 1 skein, 120 yd (109.7 m)
CC: In My Feelings; 1 skein, 120 yd (109.7 m)

Sample 2 Colors
MC: Emerald Dreams; 1 skein, 120 yds (109.7 m)
CC: Dark Cloud; 1 skein, 120 yd (109.7 m)

HOOK
6 mm (US J-10) hook, either double-ended or 2 hooks with cable at least 6 in (15 cm) long

NOTIONS
Tapestry needle, removable stitch marker

GAUGE
15 Tks and 15 rows per 4 in (10 cm)

FINISHED SIZE
A: 8 in (20 cm)
B: 28 in (70 cm)

STITCHES AND TECHNIQUES
Tss, Tks, Tks2Tog, Trs, Twup, Twks, Tunisian crochet in the round

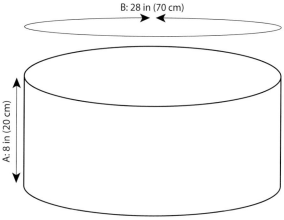

B: 28 in (70 cm)

A: 8 in (20 cm)

INSTRUCTIONS

Foundation Row: Ch 108. Starting in the 2nd ch from hook, pick up a loop in the back bump of all chains. For a longer cowl, add multiples of 36 stitches and increase number of repeats.

Foundation Row RP: Work a standard in the round return pass with MC.

Note: *A second strand of MC is required for the Foundation Row RP.*

Rnd 1: Being careful not to twist, join with Tss to first stitch of the Foundation Row and place stitch marker. Trs 107. *108 sts.*

Rnd 1 RP: For this and all remaining RP unless stated otherwise, work a standard in the round return pass.

Rnd 2: Tss 108. Fasten off MC RP strand after completing Rnd 2 RP.

Rnd 3: Trs 108. Use CC for Return Pass starting at the beginning of Rnd 3.

Rnds 4–11: *Tks 18, [Tss, Twup] 9 times. Rep from * 2 more times.

Rnd 12: *Tks, sk st, Tks 14, sk st, Tks, [Tss, Twup] 4 times, (Tks, Tss), (Twup, Twks), [Tss, Twup] 4 times. Rep from * 2 more times.

Note: *In Rnds 13–18, the Tfs stitches are used as increases between 2 Tks stitches.*

Rnd 13: *Tks, sk st, Tks 12, sk st, Tks, [Tss, Twup] 4 times, Tks, Tfs, Tks 2, Tfs, Tks, [Tss, Twup] 4 times. Rep from * 2 more times.

Rnd 14: *Tks, sk st, Tks 10, sk st, Tks, [Tss, Twup] 4 times, Tks, Tfs, Tks 4, Tfs, Tks, [Tss, Twup] 4 times. Rep from * 2 more times.

Rnd 15: *Tks, sk st, Tks 8, sk st, Tks, [Tss, Twup] 4 times, Tks, Tfs, Tks 6, Tfs, Tks, [Tss, Twup] 4 times. Rep from * 2 more times.

Rnd 16: *Tks, sk st, Tks 6, sk st, Tks, [Tss, Twup] 4 times, Tks, Tfs, Tks 8, Tfs, Tks, [Tss, Twup] 4 times. Rep from * 2 more times.

Rnd 17: *Tks, sk st, Tks 4, sk st, Tks, [Tss, Twup] 4 times, Tks, Tfs, Tks 10, Tfs, Tks, [Tss, Twup] 4 times. Rep from * 2 more times.

Rnd 18: *Tks, sk st, Tks 2, sk st, Tks, [Tss, Twup] 4 times, Tks, Tfs, Tks 12, Tfs, Tks, [Tss, Twup] 4 times. Rep from * 2 more times.

Rnd 19: *Tks2Tog 2, [Tss, Twup] 4 times, Tks, Tfs, Tks 14, Tfs, Tks, [Tss, Twup] 4 times. Rep from * 2 more times.

Rnds 20–26: *[Tss, Twup] 5 times, Tks 18, [Tss, Twup] 4 times. Rep from * 2 more times.

Note: *Rnd 27 is a partial row to create a nicer-looking border.*

Rnd 27: [Tss, Twup] 5 times. Move stitch marker to next unworked st.

Rnd 27 RP: Work a standard return pass with CC. At end of RP, drop CC and use MC for the RP for the remainder of the cowl.

Rnd 28: *Tks 18, [Tss, Twup] 9 times. Rep from * 2 more times.

Rnd 29: Trs 108.

Rnd 30: Tss 108.

Bind off: SlstBO with Trs. Fasten off.

Finishing

Use starting tail to sew Foundation Row gap closed. Weave in ends. Block to measurements.

Intrepid Capelet

The Intrepid Capelet is somewhere between a large cowl and a poncho. The capelet is worked from the bottom up and highlights the fabulous colorwork possibilities unique to Tunisian crochet in the round. Swatching for gauge is critical to getting a proper fit. If you can't simultaneously get both stitch and row gauge, use the hook size that gets the right stitch gauge and then add or subtract rows to compensate for not making the row gauge.

YARN
Malabrigo Rios; 100% Superwash Merino (Worsted weight); 210 yd (192 m) per 3.5 oz (100 g)

Colors
C1: 211 Syrah Grapes; 2 (2, 3, 3) skeins; 400 (420, 600, 630) yd / 365 (384, 549, 576) m
C2: 212 Gris; 2 (2, 3, 3) skeins; 400 (420, 600, 630) yd / 365 (384, 549, 576) m

HOOK
6.5 mm (US K-10.5) Tunisian crochet hook with cable at least 12 in (30 cm) long

6.5 mm (US K-10.5) double-ended hook (2 hooks with cable recommended)

NOTIONS
Tapestry needle, removable stitch marker

GAUGE
7 reps of [Tss, Tps] and 14 rows per 4 in (10 cm)

FINISHED SIZE
Size 1 (2, 3, 4)
A: 14 (14, 16, 16) in/35 (35, 40, 40) cm
B: 24 (26, 28, 30) in/60 (65, 70, 75) cm
C: 57 (70, 77, 88) in/143 (175, 193, 220) cm

STITCHES AND TECHNIQUES
Tss, Tks, Tps, Trs, Tx, Twup

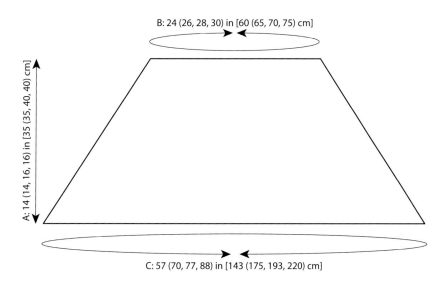

B: 24 (26, 28, 30) in [60 (65, 70, 75) cm]

A: 14 (14, 16, 16) in [35 (35, 40, 40) cm]

C: 57 (70, 77, 88) in [143 (175, 193, 220) cm]

Tunisian cross stitch (Tx): This is a stitch worked over the next 2 stitches. Skip the next set of vertical bars and Tss into the second set, and then Tss in the first set of vertical bars.

Return pass notation: This design uses decreases in the return pass. To simplify visually, a new notation will be used on return passes that have decreases.

R (standard return pass st): Yo and pull through 2 loops.

R2Tog (decrease 2 sts together): Yo and pull through 3 loops.

INSTRUCTIONS

Foundation Row: Using the hook with cable and C1, ch 201 [245, 271, 311]. Starting in the 2nd ch from hook, pick up a loop in the back bump of all chains. *201 [245, 271, 311] sts.*

Foundation Row RP: Ch 1, [yo and pull through 2 loops] rep until 2 loops rem on hook. Drop C1, pick up C2. Yo and pull through all loops.

Place marker in loop on hook (move up each round to mark start of round). Switch to double-ended hook.

Note: *C2 will now be used for all forward passes. C1 will be used for all return passes.*

Rnd 1: With C2, Trs. Being careful not to twist, join with Tks to marked st.

Rnd 1 RP: For this and all following RP unless stated otherwise, work a standard in the round RP with C1.

Rnd 2: Tks.

Rnd 3: Tks.

Rnd 4: Trs.

Rnds 5–7: Rep Rnds 2–4.

Rnd 8: [Tss, Tps] rep.

Rnd 9: [Tps, Tss] rep.

Rep Rnds 8–9 2 [2, 3, 3] more times (photo 1).

Rnd 10: [Tss, Tps] rep.

Rnd 11: Trs.

Rnds 12–17: Rep Rnds 2–7.

Rnd 18: Tx until 1 st rem, Tx in last st of rnd and first st of next rnd.

Note: *Move the stitch marker up such that it aligns vertically with the beginning of Rnd 17.*

Rnd 19: Tx.

Rep Rnds 18–19 2 [2, 3, 3] more times (photo 2).

Rnd 20: Rep Rnd 18.

Rnd 20 RP (Sizes 1, 3, 4): R, [R 3, R2Tog] rep until end.

Rnd 20 RP (Size 2 only): R 5, [R 3, R2Tog] rep until end.

Note: *Each time 2 stitches are decreased together on return pass, they are worked as a single stitch in the next round.*

Rnds 21–26: Rep Rnds 11–16. *161 [197, 217, 249] sts.*

Rnd 27: [Yo, Trs 2, pull yo over last 2 loops] rep until 1 st rem, yo, Trs into last st of rnd, Trs into first st of next rnd. Pull yo over last 2 loops (photos 3–6).

Yarn over

Work next 2 stitches.

Pull yo over last 2 stitches.

Rnd 28: [Yo, Tss 2, pull yo over last 2 loops].

Rnd 29: [Yo, Tss 2, pull yo over last 2 loops] rep until 1 st rem, yo, Tss into last st of rnd, Tss into first st of next rnd. Pull yo over last 2 loops.

Rep Rnds 28–29 2 [2, 3, 3] more times.

Rnd 30: Rep Rnd 28.

Rnd 30 RP (All sizes): R, [R 2, R2Tog] rep to end.

Rnds 31–36: Rep Rnds 11–16. *121 [148, 163, 187] sts.*

Rnd 37: Rep Rnd 17.

Rnd 37 RP (Size 1): [R2Tog, R 2, R2Tog, R] 10 times, [R2Tog, R] 17 times.

Rnd 37 RP (Size 2): [R2Tog 2, R] 13 times, [R2Tog, R] 6 times, [R2Tog 2, R] 13 times.

Rnd 37 RP (Size 3): R2Tog, R, [R2Tog 2, R] rep to end.

Rnd 37 RP (Size 4): R2Tog 3, R, [R2Tog 4, R] rep to end.

Rnds 38–40: [Tss, Twup]. *84 [90, 98, 104] sts.*
Fasten off C1.

Bind off: With C2, slstBO with [Tss, Twup]. Fasten off C2.

Finishing

Using the yarn tail, sew the Foundation Row gap closed. Weave in all ends; block gently to dimensions shown in schematic.

Moonlight Wrap

This wrap is the opposite of what many people picture when they think of Tunisian crochet. Made with DK weight yarn, the Moonlight Wrap is light, airy, and a great introduction to Tunisian crochet lace. It uses a large hook for oodles of drape and has just a six-row repeat. Creating a lace fabric requires being comfortable reading stitches. Because a larger hook is used, the stitches are looser and can be difficult to read. Gauge is also more difficult to describe. The fabric should have lots of drape and absolutely no curl. When the pattern is finished, vigorous blocking is required to open up the lace motif.

YARN

Magpie Fibers Swanky DK (DK weight); 80% Superwash Merino, 10% cashmere, 10% nylon; 250 yd (229 m) per 4.1 oz (115 g)

Color: Smoke on the Water; 3 skeins, 750 yd (686 m)

HOOK

8 mm (US L-11) Tunisian crochet hook with cable at least 12 in (30 cm) long

NOTIONS

Tapestry needle, removable stitch marker

GAUGE

10 Tss and 10 rows per 4 in (10 cm)

With a lace design, getting good drape is more important than gauge. The fabric should have no curl and lots of drape even without blocking.

FINISHED SIZE

A: 20 in (50 cm)
B: 80 in (300 cm)

STITCHES AND TECHNIQUES

Tss, Tss2Tog, Tss3Tog, Tks, Te

Double yarn over (yo 2): Yo twice. On the return pass, treat the two yo's as separate stitches.
Tss-slst: Insert hook into next st as for Tss, yo and pull through st and 1 loop on hook.

MODIFICATIONS

For a wider wrap, add multiples of 24 to the starting chain and work more repeats of the section in brackets [ ]. For a longer wrap, work extra repeats of Rows 3–8.

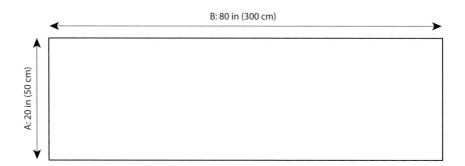

B: 80 in (300 cm)

A: 20 in (50 cm)

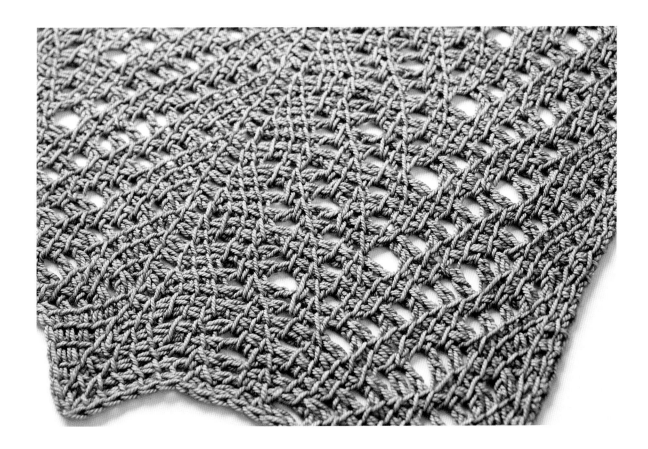

INSTRUCTIONS

Foundation Row: Ch 52. Starting in the 2nd ch from hook, pick up a loop in the back bump of all chains. *52 sts.*

Foundation Row RP: For this and all following RP, work a standard RP.

Note: All rows have 52 sts. The part of the row in [ ] is always repeated twice.

Row 1: Tss, [Tss2Tog, Tss 4, yo, Tss, Tss2Tog, yo, Tss, Tss2Tog, yo 2, Tss2Tog, Tss, yo, Tss2Tog, Tss, yo, Tss 4, Tss2Tog] twice, Tss, Te.

*Note: In Row 2, there is both a **Tks** and a **Tss** (bolded) worked into the double yo.*

Row 2: Tss, [Tss2Tog, Tss 3, yo, Tks, Tss2Tog, yo, Tks, Tss 2, **Tks**, **Tss**, Tss 2, Tks, yo, Tss2Tog, Tks, yo, Tss 3, Tss2Tog] twice, Tss, Te.

Row 3: Tss, [Tss2Tog, Tss 2, yo, Tks, Tss2Tog, yo 2, Tks, Tss3Tog, yo, Tss 2, yo, Tss3Tog, Tks, yo 2, Tss2Tog, Tks, yo, Tss 2, Tss2Tog] twice, Tss, Te.

*Note: In Row 4, there is both a **yo**, **sk st** and a **Tks** (bolded) worked into the double yo.*

Row 4: Tss, [Tss 3, Tks, Tss 2, **yo**, **sk st**, **Tks**, Tss 2, Tks, Tss 2, Tks, Tss 2, **Tks**, **yo**, **sk st**, Tss 2, Tks, Tss 3] twice, Tss, Te.

Row 5: Tss, [Tss2Tog, Tss, yo, Tss, Tss2Tog, yo, Tks, Tss, Tss2Tog, yo, Tss 4, yo, Tss2Tog, Tss, Tks, yo, Tss2Tog, Tss, yo, Tss, Tss2Tog] twice, Tss, Te.

Row 6: Tss, [Tss 2, Tks, Tss 2, Tks, Tss 3, Tks, Tss 4, Tks, Tss 3, Tks, Tss 2, Tks, Tss 2] twice, Tss, Te.

Row 7: Tss, [Tss2Tog, yo, Tss 2, Tss2Tog, yo, Tss, Tss2Tog, yo, Tss, Tss2Tog, yo 2, Tss2Tog, Tss, yo, Tss2Tog, Tss, yo, Tss2Tog, Tss 2, yo, Tss2Tog] twice, Tss, Te.

*Note: In Row 8, there is both a **Tks** and a **Tss** (bolded) worked into the double yo.*

Row 8: Tss, [Tks2Tog, Tss 3, yo, Tks, Tss2Tog, yo, Tks, Tss 2, **Tks**, **Tss**, Tss 2, Tks, yo, Tss2Tog, Tks, yo, Tss 3, Tks, Tss-slst] twice, Tss, Te.

Rows 9–200: Rep Rows 3–8 32 times or until desired length.

Note: It can be helpful to use a removable stitch marker to mark the first row of a repeat.

Rows 201–204: Rep Rows 3–6.

Row 205: Tss, [Tss2Tog, yo, Tss 2, Tss2Tog, yo, Tss, Tss2Tog, yo, Tss 6, yo, Tss2Tog, Tss, yo, Tss2Tog, Tss 2, yo, Tss2Tog] twice, Tss, Te.

Row 206: Tss, [Tks2Tog, Tss 3, yo, Tks, Tss2Tog, yo, Tks, Tss 6, Tks, yo, Tss2Tog, Tks, yo, Tss 3, Tks, Tss-slst] twice, Tss, Te.

Row 207: Tss, [Tss2Tog, Tss 2, yo, Tks, Tss2Tog, yo 2, Tks, Tss2Tog, Tss 4, Tss2Tog, Tks, yo 2, Tss2Tog, Tks, yo, Tss 2, Tss2Tog] twice, Tss, Te.

Note: *In Row 208, there is both a **yo**, **sk st** and a **Tks** (bolded) worked into the double yo.*

Row 208: Tss, [Tss 3, Tks, Tss 2, **yo**, **sk st**, **Tks**, Tss 8, **Tks**, **yo**, **sk st**, Tss 2, Tks, Tss 3] twice, Tss, Te.

Row 209: Tss, [Tss2Tog, Tss, yo, Tss, Tss2Tog, yo, Tks, Tss 10, Tks, yo, Tss2Tog, Tss, yo, Tss, Tss2Tog] twice, Tss, Te.

Bind off: Bind off loosely with scBO in the following pattern: Tss, [Tss 2, Tks, Tss 2, Tks, Tss 12,Tks, Tss 2, Tks, Tss 2] twice, Tss, Te.

Finishing

Weave in all ends. Block vigorously to open up the lace.

Sunset Lace Shawl

Create a bespoke, special occasion accessory with this semicircular lace shawl. The Sunset Lace Shawl has a radiating lace design that utilizes several techniques already used along with fading between skeins and a special bind-off. The lace pattern creates an expanding sunset motif, and the special bind-off allows for edge shaping during blocking. This shawl requires patience and attention to detail, but once you master it, you'll be ready for any Tunisian crochet adventure.

YARN

Less Traveled Yarn Paloma (Fingering weight); 90% Superwash Merino, 10% silk; 463 yd (423 m) per 3.5 oz (100 g)

Colors
C1: Desert Marigold; 1 skein, 200 yd (183 m)
C2: Poetic Peri; 1 skein, 463 yd (423 m)
C3: Cactus Flower; 1 skein, 463 yd (423 m)

HOOK

6 mm (US J-10) hook with cable at least 16 in (40 cm) long

NOTIONS

Tapestry needle

GAUGE

16 Tss and 16 rows per 4 in (10 cm)

Gauge is not critical. The fabric should have plenty of drape but not be so open you can't read the stitches.

FINISHED SIZE

A: 30 in (75 cm)
B: 70 in (180 cm)

STITCHES AND TECHNIQUES

MR, Tss, Tss2Tog, Tss3Tog, Tks, Te

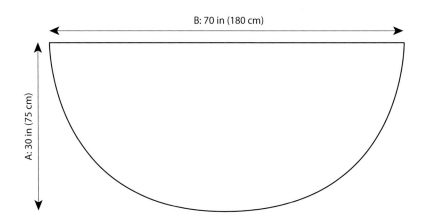

A: 30 in (75 cm)

B: 70 in (180 cm)

INSTRUCTIONS

Foundation Row: With C1, [insert hook into MR, pull up a loop, ch 1] 6 times. *6 sts.*

Foundation Row RP and all following RP: Work a standard RP.

Row 1: Yo, [Tss, yo] 4, Te. *11 sts.*

Row 2: [Tks, Tss] 4, Tks, Te. *11 sts.*

Row 3: Tss 9, Te. *11 sts.*

Row 4: [Tss, yo] 8, Tss, Te. *19 sts.*

Row 5: [Tss, Tks] 8, Tss, Te. *19 sts.*

Row 6: Tss across, Te. *19 sts.*

Note: *When there are 2 yo's together (double yo), treat them as 2 separate stitches for the return pass.*

Row 7: Tss, [yo, Tss, yo] 15 times, Tss, Te. *49 sts.*

Note: *Double yo's in Row 7 (and all rows until Row 31) are worked with both a Tks and a yo.*

Row 8: Tss, Tks, Tss, Tks, [yo, Tss, yo, Tks, Tss, Tks] 7 times, Tss, Te. *49 sts.*

Row 9: Tss, [yo, Tss3Tog, yo, Tks, Tss, Tks] 7 times, yo, Tss3Tog, yo, Tss, Te. *49 sts.*

Row 10: Tss, [Tks, Tss, Tks, Tss 3] 7 times, Tks, Tss, Tks, Tss, Te. *49 sts.*

Row 11: Tss, [yo, Tss 3, yo] 15 times, Tss, Te. *79 sts.*

Row 12: Tss, [Tks, Tss 3, Tks, yo, Tss 3, yo] 7 times, Tks, Tss 3, Tks, Tss, Te.

Row 13: Tss, yo, [Tss, Tss3Tog, Tss, yo 2, Tks, Tss3Tog, Tks, yo 2] 7 times, Tss, Tss3Tog, Tss, yo, Tss, Te.

Rows 14–15: Rep Rows 12–13.

Row 16: Rep Row 12.

Row 17: Tss, [yo, Tss 5, yo 2, Tks, Tss 3, Tks, yo] 7 times, yo, Tss 5, yo, Tss, Te. *109 sts.*

Row 18: Tss, [Tks, Tss 5, Tks, yo, Tss 5, yo] 7 times, Tks, Tss 5, Tks, Tss, Te.

Row 19: Tss, yo, [Tss 2, Tss3Tog, Tss 2, yo 2, Tks, Tss, Tss3Tog, Tss, Tks, yo 2] 7 times, Tss 2, Tss3Tog, Tss 2, yo, Tss, Te.

Rows 20–23: Rep Rows 18–19.

Row 24: Rep Row 18.

Row 25: Tss, [yo, Tss 7, yo 2, Tks, Tss 5, Tks, yo] 7 times, yo, Tss 7, yo, Tss, drop C1, pick up C2, Te. *139 sts.*

Row 26: Tss, [Tks, Tss 7, Tks, yo, Tss 7, yo] 7 times, Tks, Tss 7, Tks, Tss, drop C2, pick up C1, Te.

Row 27: Tss, yo, [Tss 3, Tss3Tog, Tss 3, yo 2, Tks, Tss 2, Tss3Tog, Tss 2, Tks, yo 2] 7 times, Tss 3, Tss3Tog, Tss 3, yo, Tss, drop C1, pick up C2, Te.

Rows 28–31: Rep Rows 26–27.

Note: *Starting in Row 32, all double yo's have both a Tks and a Tss worked into them.*

Row 32: Tss, Tks, [Tss 7, Tks, Tss] 15 times, drop C2, pick up C1, Te.

Row 33: Tss, [yo, Tss 4, yo, Tss2Tog, Tss 3, yo] 15 times, Tss, drop C1, pick up C2, Te. *169 sts.*

Row 34: Tss, Tks, [Tss 4, Tks, Tss 4, Tks, Tss] 15 times, drop C2, pick up C1, Te.

Row 35: Tss, [yo, Tss 2, Tss2Tog, yo, Tss3Tog, yo, Tss2Tog, Tss 2, yo] 15 times, Tss, drop C1, pick up C2, Te.

Row 36: Tss, Tks, [Tss 3, Tks, Tss, Tks, Tss 3, Tks, Tss] 15 times, drop C2, pick up C1, Te.

Row 37: Tss, [yo, Tss, Tss2Tog, yo, Tss, Tss3Tog, Tss, yo, Tss2Tog, Tss, yo] 15 times, Tss, drop C1, pick up C2, Te.

Row 38: Tss, Tks, [Tss 2, Tks, Tss 3, Tks, Tss 2, Tks, Tss] 15 times, drop C2, pick up C1, Te.

Row 39: Tss, [yo, Tss2Tog, yo, Tss 2, Tss3Tog, Tss 2, yo, Tss2Tog, yo] 15 times, Tss, drop C1, pick up C2, Te. Fasten off C1.

Row 40: Tss, Tks, [Tss, Tks, Tss 5, Tks, Tss, Tks, Tss] 15 times, Te.

Row 41: Tss, [yo, Tss 5, yo, Tss2Tog, Tss 4, yo] 15 times, Tss, Te. *199 sts.*

Row 42: Tss, Tks, [Tss 5, Tks, Tss 5, Tks, Tss] 15 times, Te.

Row 43: Tss, [yo, Tss 3, Tss2Tog, yo, Tss3Tog, yo, Tss2Tog, Tss 3, yo] 15 times, Tss, Te.

Row 44: Tss, Tks, [Tss 4, Tks, Tss, Tks, Tss 4, Tks, Tss] 15 times, Te.

Row 45: Tss, [yo, Tss 2, Tss2Tog, yo, Tss, Tss3Tog, Tss, yo, Tss2Tog, Tss 2, yo] 15 times, Tss, Te.

Row 46: Tss, Tks, [Tss 3, Tks, Tss 3, Tks, Tss 3, Tks, Tss] 15 times, Te.

Row 47: Tss, [yo, Tss, Tss2Tog, yo, Tss 2, Tss3Tog, Tss 2, yo, Tss2Tog, Tss, yo] 15 times, Tss, Te.

Row 48: Tss, Tks, [Tss 2, Tks, Tss 5, Tks, Tss, Tks, Tss 2, Tks, Tss] 15 times, Te.

Row 49: Tss, [yo, Tss, Tss2Tog, yo, Tss 7, yo, Tss2Tog, Tss, yo] 15 times, Tss, Te. *229 sts.*

Row 50: Tss, Tks, [Tss 2, Tks, Tss 7, Tks, Tss 2, Tks, Tss] 15 times, Te.

Row 51: Tss, [yo, Tss 5, Tss3Tog, yo, Tss2Tog, Tss 5, yo] 15 times, Tss, Te.

Row 52: Tss, Tks, [Tss 6, Tks, Tss 6, Tks, Tss] 15 times, Te.

Row 53: Tss, [yo, Tss 4, Tss2Tog, yo, Tss3Tog, yo, Tss2Tog, Tss 4, yo] 15 times, Tss, Te.

Row 54: Tss, Tks, [Tss 5, Tks, Tss, Tks, Tss 5, Tks, Tss] 15 times, Te.

Row 55: Tss, [yo, Tss 3, Tss2Tog, yo, Tss, Tss3Tog, Tss, yo, Tss2Tog, Tss 3, yo] 15 times, Tss, Te.

Row 56: Tss, Tks, [Tss 4, Tks, Tss 3, Tks, Tss 4, Tks, Tss] 15 times, Te.

Row 57: Tss, [yo, Tss 3, Tss2Tog, yo, Tss 5, yo, Tss2Tog, Tss 3, yo] 15 times, Tss, drop C2, pick up C3, Te. *259 sts.*

Row 58: Tss, Tks, [Tss 4, Tks, Tss 5, Tks, Tss 4, Tks, Tss] 15 times, drop C3, pick up C2, Te.

Row 59: Tss, [yo, Tss 2, Tss2Tog, yo, Tss 3, Tss3Tog, Tss 3, yo, Tss2Tog, Tss 2, yo] 15 times, Tss, drop C2, pick up C3, Te.

Row 60: Tss, Tks, [Tss 3, Tks, Tss 7, Tks, Tss 3, Tks, Tss] 15 times, drop C3, pick up C2, Te.

Row 61: Tss, [yo, Tss, Tss2Tog, yo, Tss 4, Tss3Tog, Tss 4, yo, Tss2Tog, Tss, yo] 15 times, Tss, drop C2, pick up C3, Te.

Row 62: Tss, Tks, [Tss 2, Tks, Tss 9, Tks, Tss 2, Tks, Tss] 15 times, drop C3, pick up C2, Te.

Row 63: Tss, [yo, Tss2Tog, yo, Tss 5, Tss3Tog, Tss 5, yo, Tss2Tog, yo] 15 times, Tss, drop C2, pick up C3, Te.

Row 64: Tss, Tks, [Tss, Tks, Tss 11, Tks, Tss, Tks, Tss] 15 times, drop C3, pick up C2, Te.

Row 65: Tss, [yo, Tss 6, Tss2Tog, yo, Tss, yo, Tss2Tog, Tss 6, yo] 15 times, Tss, drop C2, pick up C3, Te. *289 sts.*

Row 66: Tss, Tks, [Tss 7, Tks, Tss, Tks, Tss 7, Tks, Tss] 15 times, drop C3, pick up C2, Te.

Row 67: Tss, [yo, Tss 5, Tss2Tog, yo, Tss3Tog, yo, Tss2Tog, yo, Tss2Tog, Tss 5, yo] 15 times, Tss, drop C2, pick up C3, Te.

Row 68: Tss, Tks, [Tss 6, [Tks, Tss] 3 times, Tss 5, Tks, Tss] 15 times, drop C3, pick up C2, Te.

Row 69: Tss, *yo, Tss 4, [Tss2Tog, yo] twice, Tss3Tog, [yo, Tss2Tog] twice, Tss 4, yo; rep from * 15 times, Tss, drop C2, pick up C3, Te.

Row 70: Tss, Tks, *Tss 5, [Tks, Tss] 4 times, Tss 4, Tks, Tss; rep from * 15 times, drop C3, pick up C2, Te.

Row 71: Tss, *yo, Tss 3, [Tss2Tog, yo] twice, Tss3Tog, [yo, Tss2Tog] 3 times, Tss 3, yo; rep from * 15 times, Tss, drop C2, pick up C3, Te. Fasten off C2.

Row 72: Tss, Tks, *Tss 4, [Tks, Tss] 5 times, Tss 3, Tks, Tss; rep from * 15 times, Te.

Row 73: Tss, *yo, Tss 3, [Tss2Tog, yo] 3 times, Tss, [yo, Tss2Tog] 3 times, Tss 3, yo; rep from * 15 times, Tss, Te. *319 sts.*

Row 74: Tss, Tks, *Tss 4, [Tks, Tss] 6 times, Tss 3, Tks, Tss; rep from * 15 times, Te.

Row 75: Tss, *yo, Tss 2, [Tss2Tog, yo] 3 times, Tss3Tog, [yo, Tss2Tog] 4 times, Tss 2, yo; rep from * 15 times, Tss, Te.

Row 76: Tss, Tks, *Tss 3, [Tks, Tss] 7 times, Tss 2, Tks, Tss; rep from * 15 times, Te.

Row 77: Tss, *yo, Tss, [Tss2Tog, yo] 4 times, Tss3Tog, [yo, Tss2Tog] 4 times, Tss, yo; rep from * 15 times, Tss, Te.

Row 78: Tss, Tks, *Tss 2, [Tks, Tss] 8 times, Tss, Tks, Tss; rep from * 15 times, Te.

Row 79: Tss, *yo, [Tss2Tog, yo] 4 times, Tss3Tog, [yo, Tss2Tog] 5 times, yo; rep from * 15 times, Tss, Te.

Row 80: Tss, Tks, *Tss, [Tks, Tss] 10 times; rep from * 15 times, Te.

Row 81: Tss, yo, *yo, [Tss2Tog, yo] 5 times, Tss, [yo, Tss2Tog] 5 times, yo 2; rep from * 15 times, Tss, Te. *365 sts.*

Note: *The bind-off is a bit unusual because this shawl will need to be blocked aggressively to open up the lace. There is a slstBO for the first Tss and last 2 stitches. The remainder of the bind-off is working a slstBO Tks with a ch1 into all the yo sts and skipping all the other sts. For the yo 3, you work 3 (slstBO Tks, ch 1) into the same space.*

Bind off: SlstBO Tss, (slstBO Tks, ch1, slstBO Tks, ch1) in yo 2, skipping all non-yo spaces, [(slstBO Tks, ch1) 10, (slstBO Tks, ch1) 3 in yo 3] 14 times, (slstBO Tks, ch1) 10, (slstBO Tks, ch1) twice in yo 2, slstBO Tss, slstBO Te.

Finishing

Weave in all ends. Block aggressively and use pins to create peaks at the yo 3.

Resources

I'd like to extend my heartfelt thanks to all these yarn makers/dyers for providing the beautiful and squishy yarn to make this book happen.

- Cascade Yarns (cascadeyarns.com)
- Birch Hollow Fibers (birchhollowfibers.com)
- Camellia Fiber Company (camelliafibercompany.com)
- Kim Dyes Yarn (kimdyesyarn.com)
- KnittinBro (knittinbro.com)
- Lolabean Yarn Co. (lolabeanyarnco.com)
- Madeline Tosh (madelinetosh.com)
- Magpie Fibers (magpiefibers.com)
- Malabrigo (malabrigoyarn.com)
- Marianated Yarns (marianatedyarns.com)
- Seismic Yarn (seismicyarn.com)

References

Grabowski, Angela. *Encyclopedia of Tunisian Crochet*. Abilene, TX: LoneStar Abilene Publishing, 2004.

Lipsey, Toni. *The Tunisian Crochet Handbook*. New York: Abrams, 2021.

Ohrenstein, Dora. *The New Tunisian Crochet*. Loveland, CO: Interweave, 2012.

Silverman, Sharon Hernes. *Tunisian Crochet*. Mechanicsburg, PA: Stackpole Books, 2009.

Acknowledgments

Many thanks to all the folks who have supported me on my journey from new designer to book author. Thanks to Amy Rooney and Marit Munson—by supporting me early in my design career, these amazing women helped motivate me to continue this journey. Along the way, so many designer friends (especially Jen and Elizabeth) have been a constant source of encouragement, commiseration, and support.

Thank you to Stefan for being an amazing photographer, occasional model, and helpful proofreader. Thank you to my amazing tech editor, Sharon, for your patience and assistance in making these patterns accurate and consistent.

A special thanks to all my amazing testers: Ann, Britt, Cecelia, Christine, Corey, Doug, Freda, Jenny, Joanna, Julie, Kayla, Kim, Kristin, Marieke, Mary, McKenna, Mia, Millie, Natalie, Rachel, Tenia, Tricia, and Virginia. Some of these folks have been testing with me since the very beginning, and many have tested for me over and over. They all provide amazing insight and community. Without these fabulous testers, this book would not be possible.

Index of Stitch Tutorials

Visual Index

DIFFICULTY LEVEL 3

DIFFICULTY LEVEL 4